365 days *of* prayer

Simple Reflections to Connect You to God

EDITORS OF GUIDEPOSTS

with Sabra Ciancanelli

Guideposts

365 Days of Prayer: Simple Reflections to Connect You to God

Published by Guideposts Books & Inspirational Media
100 Reserve Road, Suite E200
Danbury, CT 06810
Guideposts.org

Acknowledgments

Every attempt has been made to credit the sources of copyrighted material used in this book. If any such acknowledgment has been inadvertently omitted or miscredited, receipt of such information would be appreciated.

Scripture quotations marked (AKJV) are taken from the *Authorized (King James) Version of the Bible* ("the KJV"), the rights in which are vested in the Crown in the United Kingdom and are reproduced here by permission of the Crown's patentee, Cambridge University Press.

Scripture quotations marked (CEB) are taken from the *Common English Bible*. Copyright © 2011 by Common English Bible.

Scripture quotations marked (ESV) are taken from the *Holy Bible, English Standard Version*. Copyright © 2001 by Crossway Bibles, a division of Good News Publishers. Used by permission. All rights reserved.

Scripture quotations marked (GNT) are taken from the *Holy Bible, Good News Translation*. Copyright © 1992 by American Bible Society.

Scripture quotations marked (KJV) are taken from the *King James Version of the Bible*.

Scripture quotations marked (MSG) are taken from *The Message*. Copyright © 1993, 1994, 1995, 1996, 2000, 2001, 2002 by Eugene H. Peterson.

Scripture quotations marked (NASB) are taken from the *New American Standard Bible*. Copyright © 1960, 1962, 1963, 1968, 1971, 1972, 1973, 1975, 1977, 1995 by The Lockman Foundation, La Habra, California. Used by permission.

Scripture quotations marked (NCV) are taken from *The Holy Bible, New Century Version*. Copyright © 2005 by Thomas Nelson.

Scripture quotations marked (NIV) are taken from *The Holy Bible, New International Version*. Copyright © 1973, 1978, 1984, 2011 by Biblica, Inc. Used by permission of Zondervan. All rights reserved worldwide. zondervan.com

Scripture quotations marked (NKJV) are taken from *The Holy Bible,* New King James Version. Copyright © 1982 by Thomas Nelson.

Scripture quotations marked (NLT) are taken from the *Holy Bible, New Living Translation*. Copyright © 1996, 2004, 2007 by Tyndale House Foundation. Used by permission of Tyndale House Publishers Inc., Carol Stream, Illinois. All rights reserved.

Scripture quotations marked (NLV) are from the *New Life Bible,* copyright © 1969 by Christian Literature International. Used by permission. All rights reserved.

Scripture quotations marked (NRSV) are taken from the *New Revised Standard Version Bible*. Copyright © 1989 by the Division of Christian Education of the National Council of the Churches of Christ in the United States of America. Used by permission. All rights reserved.

Scripture quotations marked (RSV) are taken from the *Revised Standard Version of the Bible*. Copyright © 1946, 1952, 1971 by the Division of Christian Education of the National Council of the Churches of Christ in the United States of America. Used by permission.

Scripture quotations marked (TLB) are taken from *The Living Bible*. Copyright © 1971 by Tyndale House Publishers, Inc., Carol Stream, Illinois. All rights reserved.

Cover design by Pamela Walker, W Design Studio LLC, wdesignstudiollc.com
Interior design by Pamela Walker, W Design Studio LLC, wdesignstudiollc.com
Cover photo by Dreamstime.com
Typesetting by Aptara
Printed and bound in the United States of America
10 9 8 7 6 5 4 3 2 1

Then you will call on me
and come and pray to me,
and I will listen to you.

JEREMIAH 29:12 (NIV)

Introduction

When I tell people I write prayers for a living, I often receive a surprised look. Truth is, I fell into my career, surrendering to God to lead me to the place I was meant to be. I was in my twenties, writing the marketing materials for a plastics company, when they downsized and had to let me go. I had been out of work for weeks and was feeling miserable and lost, desperately praying for any sort of opportunity to come my way, when my old boss at the plastics place called and asked if I was interested in working for an inspirational publisher. "I heard of a job opening and it's more suited to your skills," he said. "They'll be calling you."

Unfortunately, I botched the interview. I was asked to edit a story down to a specific word count and I misheard the number, so what I handed in was an abstract, a skeleton of a story, barely a paragraph. "I see what you've done here," the managing editor said, "but Sabra, can you explain why you did it?" When I told him how much I struggled to turn three pages into the restrictive word count, he tipped his head back and laughed. A week later I got the happy news that I was part of the team.

Hired as an editor at Guideposts, I loved being immersed in people's true stories of hope and inspiration. When the opportunity arose to create prayer programs, I was intrigued. The first series I worked on was centered on the words of Jesus. The deadline was tight, so I was typing away for most of the night, the only one up in a dark house, reading and rereading Jesus's teachings, when Matthew 5:16 (NKJV) caught my attention: "Let your light so shine before men, that they may see your good works and glorify your Father in heaven."

I repeated the verse, personalizing it: *Let my light shine so that my work glorifies God.* Jesus's message came through loud and clear, and it felt perfectly meant just for me—words from above cheering me on. It was in that moment that I discovered the blessing of connecting with God and writing from the heart. From there my devotional writing developed into the devotional magazine *60 Days of Prayer* and now this book, with devotions carefully selected and edited by Morgan Beard.

When I sit down to write devotions, my intention is to be that light and inspire others to feel God's presence. It's my deepest hope that the Bible verses, reflections, and prayers in these pages will inspire you to grow closer to God and feel His love and guidance in your life, to take each day's devotion into your heart. We've included a reflections area at the bottom of each page if you'd like to record your thoughts, prayers, and experiences on these devotions.

Words cannot express how grateful I am that God has taken me on this amazing journey and how wonderful it is to be a part of your faith practice. May these devotions help you to see His grace in your life and inspire you to say yes to the magnificent opportunities and blessings that will guide you to let your light shine through your good work.

Sabra Ciancanelli
Editor, *60 Days of Prayer*

God's Blessings
Grace Your Future

*He wakens me morning by morning, wakens
my ear to listen like one being instructed.*

ISAIAH 50:4 (NIV)

God awakens you every morning, and He is there to guide you through the day. When you are weary or troubled by worries, be assured that His blessings will grace your future. The days to come will be filled with His unending love and abundance.

*Heavenly Father, awaken my ear so that
I may hear Your divine instructions.
Lift my spirit and fill me with Your joy.*

Reflections

His Steadfast Love

I will sing of the Lord's unfailing love forever! Young and old will hear of your faithfulness.

PSALM 89:1 (NLT)

God's sweet presence is woven into everyday messages of His love. Little reminders are sprinkled throughout the day—in the magnificent blue sky; in the dawn chorus of birds; in a single, heart-shaped leaf; in the perfect song on the radio—His beauty and love are all around us. Today, make it a point to take notice. His messages of love are always there.

Heavenly Father, today I will seek, see, and be grateful for the many ways You show Your love.

Reflections

Make a Breakthrough

Since they could not get him to Jesus because of the crowd, they made an opening in the roof above Jesus by digging through it and then lowered the mat the man was lying on.

MARK 2:4 (NIV)

In this scripture, a group of men were so determined to help their paralyzed friend see Jesus that they broke through the roof and lowered him down. Their breakthrough led Jesus to heal the man. Look to your heart. Is there any place where you need a breakthrough for healing?

Heavenly Father, help me identify and break down the barriers that block me from Your healing.

Reflections

Choose Your New Theme

Gracious words are like a honeycomb,
sweetness to the soul and health to the body.

PROVERBS 16:24 (ESV)

Many people select a word that becomes a theme, a meditation, and a prayer for the next day, week, month, or even year. If you'd like to try this powerful prayer exercise, sit down and pray with the intention of finding your word. Make a list of words that come to you. Perhaps you'll come up with something like *balance, patience,* or *abundance.* The possibilities are endless!

Heavenly Father, lead me to a word that will guide me
for as long as I need it. A word that will help me grow.

Reflections

Face Your Challenges

If God is for us, who can be against us?

ROMANS 8:31 (NIV)

Norman Vincent Peale developed the technique of imagining all your difficulties as an army lined up against you, and realizing you have a force at your disposal that can overcome them all. Face your enemies—discouragement, frustration, disappointment, financial trouble—and repeat the above scripture.

Heavenly Father, thank You for helping me to defeat my problems—and to not fear what lies ahead.

Reflections

In God's Care

*If I ride the wings of the morning, if I dwell by the
farthest oceans, even there your hand will guide me,
and your strength will support me.*

PSALM 139:9–10 (NLT)

This beautiful verse is a reminder that you are in God's
care. When life's journey is bumpy and uncertain, know
that you are in His hands and that He has the power,
wisdom, and strength to guide you through every situation. Visualize Him taking your hand and comforting
you with His peace.

*Dear God, because of You I will not fear any danger,
for I am in the shelter of Your wings.*

Reflections

Pray "As If"

*Devote yourselves to prayer,
being watchful and thankful.*

COLOSSIANS 4:2 (NIV)

———

There's an old saying often attributed to St. Ignatius: "Pray as if everything depends on God, work as if everything depends on you." When you pray and work with all you've got, you really can't lose. Even if you fall short of reaching your goal, you will be better for the experience.

*Dear Lord, encourage me to keep working,
keep trying, keep hoping, and keep praying.*

Reflections

Boost Your Energy

*I am come that they might have life, and that
they might have it more abundantly.*

JOHN 10:10 (KJV)

F eeling a little drained? Fill your mind with Christ. Fill
your heart with Him. Feel His energy, vitality, exuberance, delight, and eagerness well up within you. Pray for
Him to help you release life's hidden stresses and worries and restore you with His peace.

*Dear God, pick me up with Your love!
Restore me with Your infinite energy.*

Reflections

Cure for Negative News

*I have told you all this so that you may
have peace in me. Here on earth you will have many
trials and sorrows. But take heart, because
I have overcome the world.*

JOHN 16:33 (NLT)

Negative news seems to dominate the media. If we aren't careful, the negatives of the world can dominate our thinking and leave us feeling depressed and hopeless. If you feel yourself spiraling downward, and peace seems out of reach, remind yourself of this verse. Amazing powers are within us. Turn your concerns about the state of the world into prayer.

*Heavenly Father, when I am feeling helpless
and hopeless over negative news stories, I will turn
to You for prayer, hope, and wisdom.*

Reflections

Let God Flow

Set your minds on things above, not on earthly things.

COLOSSIANS 3:2 (NIV)

Is something bothering you? The secret to healing past hurts or future worries is to let God's grace flow in. Yet as easy as it sounds, "letting God" is one of the hardest things to do. Loosen your grasp of forcing the outcome that you want and know that God can handle those things that you cannot. He is with you now and wants to help. Open up and let Him in.

Dear Lord, help me let go and let You take over.
You are my very present help!

Reflections

Praise God

I will bless the Lord at all times: his praise shall continually be in my mouth.

PSALM 34:1 (KJV)

Try this powerful prayer technique: begin your prayer time with praise. Praise God for His glory and mercy and His ability to redeem every situation and convert challenges into positive growth. Praise Him for His holiness, His greatness, and His promises.

Heavenly Father, thank You for giving me so many reasons to praise You.

Reflections

From Self-Reliance to God-Confidence

*Don't be so naive and self-confident. You're not
exempt. You could fall flat on your face as easily
as anyone else. Forget about self-confidence;
it's useless. Cultivate God-confidence.*

1 CORINTHIANS 10:12 (MSG)

At one time or another, we are all guilty of making the
mistake of trusting ourselves instead of God. Perhaps
you make it when you hold onto a worry or try to answer
your own prayers. When you find yourself relying on
yourself instead of Him, shift your focus and place your
cares in His capable hands.

*Lord Jesus, help me to believe and trust that
You have everything under control.*

Reflections

Discover Unsearchable Things

Call to me and I will answer you and tell you great and unsearchable things you do not know.

JEREMIAH 33:3 (NIV)

Sometimes life can be too complicated to understand. When you feel knocked down or confused by a situation, call upon God, and He will bless you with His infinite wisdom. He offers a way to discover "unsearchable things" that can only be known by knowing Him. Only He has answers to indecipherable problems.

Heavenly Father, thank You for helping me discover unsearchable things.

Reflections

Mend a Relationship

Finally, all of you, have unity of mind, sympathy, brotherly love, a tender heart, and a humble mind.

1 PETER 3:8 (ESV)

Is there a relationship in your life that could use mending? Perhaps a friend that has drifted away or a dispute with a loved one? Mending bruised and broken relationships is Christ's work. He can go before you and make the crooked ways straight. Pray for help straightening out misunderstandings between yourself and others.

Heavenly Father, I confess my heart is not always tender and kind to those in my life. I ask You to give me the gift of Your tenderness, Your kindness and generosity of Spirit so that I can share those gifts with others.

Reflections

Best Way to Start Your Day

For his anger lasts only a moment, but his favor lasts a lifetime; weeping may stay for the night, but rejoicing comes in the morning.

PSALM 30:5 (NIV)

It's been said that the difference between a good day and a bad one depends completely on your attitude. The best way to start each day is to begin with a simple prayer. An attitude of gratitude is a decision you can make each morning.

Good morning, God. Thank You for all my blessings. Thank You for today.

Reflections

Elijah and the Ravens

*The ravens brought him bread and meat in the
morning and bread and meat in the evening,
and he drank from the brook.*

1 KINGS 17:6 (NIV)

Elijah was alone, and most likely afraid, when the
ravens first swooped down to feed him. But the ravens,
acting against their own natural impulses to scavenge
and devour food, instead did as God had promised.
Have you ever had to fight your own wants and desires
to follow God's instructions? Do you answer His calls?

*Heavenly Father, I long to serve You knowing
that You will always provide for me.*

Reflections

Breathe Prayer

Into your hands I commit my spirit.

PSALM 31:5 (NIV)

———————◆———————

When you feel frustrated about a situation, pray the above verse. Feel God's peace calming you. Ask Him to help you let go of difficult emotions. Breathe His Spirit into you and see this trying moment as an exercise in faith—of stretching your love and patience—and growing deeper and closer to Him.

*Gracious God, help me let go of control as
I breathe in Your strength and grace.*

Reflections

Do You Trust Broken Cisterns?

My people have committed two sins: They have forsaken me, the spring of living water, and have dug their own cisterns, broken cisterns that cannot hold water.

JEREMIAH 2:13 (NIV)

In the above verse, Jeremiah points out that his people are foolishly looking to the wrong things—"broken cisterns," ideas or beliefs that don't hold water, that can never truly satisfy. Jesus gives us a spring of Living Water that will never run dry.

Lord, only You can satisfy the longing in my heart.

Reflections

The Seed of His Blessings

Others, like seed sown on good soil, hear the word, accept it, and produce a crop—some thirty, some sixty, some a hundred times what was sown.

MARK 4:20 (NIV)

Ask yourself, what small things can I do to help spread the good news of Jesus? Don't overcomplicate things; simply be a messenger, a seed floating on the breeze, bringing God's Word and sharing the hope He brings to others.

Father, Your Word is alive and active. Guide me to sow Your seeds in the hearts of others.

Reflections

All Things Work for Good

*And we know that all things work together
for good to those who love God, to those who
are the called according to His purpose.*

ROMANS 8:28 (NKJV)

God has the amazing ability to turn things around.
Even terrible circumstances or emotions as difficult as
grief can bring healing. Because of His awesome power
to bring good out of bad, we do not need to be victims
of our circumstances.

*Heavenly Father, release me of what-if fears.
Give me a firm faith that trusts "all things
work together for good."*

Reflections

Enhance Your Spiritual Sight

*Then Jesus placed his hands on the man's eyes again,
and his eyes were opened. His sight was completely
restored, and he could see everything clearly.*

MARK 8:25 (NLT)

When you read the Bible, Jesus is improving your spiritual eyesight. He is opening your understanding so that you can know Him better and apply His spiritual principles to your life. If you are struggling with a challenging verse or passage, ask for His help so that you may see how to apply His Word to your life.

*Heavenly Father, heal and open my spiritual eyes
so that I may see You more clearly.*

Reflections

From Darkness to Light

The engulfing waters threatened me, the deep surrounded me ... but you, Lord my God, brought my life up from the pit. When my life was ebbing away, I remembered you, LORD.

JONAH 2:5–7 (NIV)

Imagine Jonah, in the darkness, inside the belly of the great fish, with seemingly no way to escape. His future looked hopeless, and yet God delivered him. When you feel enveloped by darkness, focus on His promises. He is the Light.

Almighty Lord, like Jonah, I know You will always bring me up from the pit. I know You won't forget me.

Reflections

Pray Your Way Through Your Day

Pray continually...

1 THESSALONIANS 5:17 (NIV)

Today's faith exercise is to pray throughout your day. Make an effort to consciously work God into your thinking. Invite Him into your mind and ask Him to show you opportunities or inspire new ideas. Reach out and invite His amazing power to manifest in your life.

Heavenly Father, I want to talk with You about everything. You are my trusted teacher and friend. You are the Source of life, knowledge, and wisdom.

Reflections

Ponder with All Your Heart

*When they had seen him, they spread the word
concerning what had been told them about this
child, and all who heard it were amazed at what the
shepherds said to them. But Mary treasured up all
these things and pondered them in her heart.*

LUKE 2:17–19 (NIV)

In the above verse, Mary is overjoyed by the miracle of
Jesus's birth. But it takes time to process all that had
happened, to fully comprehend the amazing blessing
bestowed upon the world. Today, take a moment and
do the same: reflect on the Child of Bethlehem and the
miracle of His birth.

*Merciful God, thank You for living
among us, as one of us.*

Reflections

Accept God's Forgiveness

*Therefore, there is now no condemnation
for those who are in Christ Jesus.*

ROMANS 8:1 (NIV)

Is there something that you've done that you just can't
get over? Confess your sin to God and know that God
longs to transform your life through the grace of His
forgiveness. Feel the weight of regret leave your heart.

*Heavenly Father, I seek Your forgiveness. Help me
grow from this experience so that I can be more
compassionate and forgiving to others.*

Reflections

The Best Advice

But Rehoboam rejected the advice the elders gave him and consulted the young men who had grown up with him and were serving him.

1 KINGS 12:8 (NIV)

God gave us His Spirit to nudge us in ways we can't always explain—a gut feeling, a phone call at exactly the right time, an email subject line that speaks directly to our problem. When we immerse ourselves in the Word of God, we grow more connected to Him, and it becomes easier to know when He is leading us.

Heavenly Father, You always speak to me when I need guidance. You are the best counsel I can have.

Reflections

Unfreeze Your Heart

Judge not, that you be not judged.

MATTHEW 7:1 (ESV)

Sometimes we make the mistake of freezing people in time. We remember them at their worst moments and don't give them a second chance or have faith that they can change. In God's grace, we can let go of our assumptions about people and open our hearts to see others as Christ sees them.

Heavenly Father, help me to let go of thoughts of others that are frozen in time. Unfreeze my heart.

Reflections

Time for a Change

Do not conform to the pattern of this world, but be transformed by the renewing of your mind. Then you will be able to test and approve what God's will is— his good, pleasing and perfect will.

ROMANS 12:2 (NIV)

D o you feel a need to renew your mind? Listen to the voice deep in your heart and be guided by God's wisdom. Steer away from things that give you that nagging negative feeling in the pit of your stomach, and make habits and choices that lead you toward your best life.

Heavenly Father, You are my guide. Help me live a life that frees me from discomfort. Help me make choices that please You.

Reflections

Little Things

His master said to him, "Well done, good and faithful servant. You have been faithful over a little; I will set you over much. Enter into the joy of your master."

MATTHEW 25:21 (ESV)

The parable of the good and faithful servant in Matthew emphasizes the value of little things. Sometimes we think in grandiose terms: What bold, grand gesture can we make to show our faith? But in this parable, as well as in the life of Jesus, it is the little things that help you "enter into the joy of your Master."

*Heavenly Father, guide me to the little things
I can do right now.*

Reflections

God's Healing Power

O Lord, if you heal me, I will be truly healed; if you save me, I will be truly saved. My praises are for you alone!

JEREMIAH 17:14 (NLT)

D₀ you need to feel God's healing power? Make time for yourself and for God. Pray and ask Him to help you relax so that you receive His divine healing. Share your fears and tears. Ask that He shine His blessings on you.

Heavenly Father, I seek Your calming peace that comes from the wisdom that "this too shall pass."

Reflections

Shine for Jesus

*In the same way, let your light shine before others,
that they may see your good deeds and glorify
your Father in heaven.*

MATTHEW 5:16 (NIV)

One of the purest forms of devotion is service—doing God's work on earth. By bringing happiness, peace, and security to others, we bring His heavenly traits to earth. When we serve others, we serve Christ.

Our Heavenly Father, help me to live so that I not only have strength and joy myself, but that I may help others and build Your kingdom on earth.

Reflections

FEB
1

DAY
32

God Looks to the Heart

*For God does not see as man sees, since man
looks at the outward appearance, but the
Lord looks at the heart.*

1 SAMUEL 16:7 (NASB)

Wе live in a world obsessed with outward appearance, but the beautiful truth is that God's focus is on the inside. Take some time to look inward and spend time developing something that will last for all eternity—your relationship with Him.

*Heavenly Father, help me to remember
that true beauty comes from within.*

Reflections

Follow the Leader

Am I now trying to win the approval of human beings, or of God? Or am I trying to please people? If I were still trying to please people, I would not be a servant of Christ.

GALATIANS 1:10 (NIV)

In this scripture, the apostle Paul addresses a problem everyone faces at one time or another: Do we please the people around us, or do we please God? Your life won't always make sense and you won't always make others happy, but it's best to decide to trust His plan and purpose for your life. Seek to please and obey God over other people, and everything else will fall into place.

Heavenly Father, I come to You today with a heart open and ready to follow You.

Reflections

The Salt of the Earth

You are the salt of the earth. But if the salt loses its saltiness, how can it be made salty again? It is no longer good for anything, except to be thrown out and trampled underfoot.

MATTHEW 5:13 (NIV)

While preaching the Sermon on the Mount, Jesus proclaimed, "You are the salt of the earth." On the simplest level, Christ's words are about salt as a flavor enhancer. He is telling us that as Christians, we are here to season the world with grace and the good things that result from our knowing Him.

Lord Jesus, today and every day, help me be full of grace and salt.

Reflections

Working with God

*I am come that they might have life, and that
they might have it more abundantly.*

JOHN 10:10 (AKJV)

No matter what your occupation, you will always have
more success when you include the Lord. Take Him as
your partner and you will discover new power, strength,
and perspective. Your attitude will brighten and your
efforts will be rewarded.

*Lord, You are my partner, an ever-present Source
of guidance and wisdom. Make our plans BIG.*

Reflections

The Power of Fasting

And when you fast, don't make it obvious, as the hypocrites do... when you fast, comb your hair and wash your face. Then no one will notice that you are fasting, except your Father, who knows what you do in private.

MATTHEW 6:16–18 (NLT)

Fasting—giving up something in order to focus on God—can draw us closer to Jesus, but only if we can do it without drawing attention to ourselves. Jesus warns us to keep our fasting private so that we can focus on Him and discover the root of our needs, which Jesus can then step in and meet.

Heavenly Father, today I will give up something that I consume mindlessly—social media, television, snacking—and focus on You.

Reflections

Get in God's Groove

*I'll show you how to take a real rest. Walk with
me and work with me—watch how I do it.
Learn the unforced rhythms of grace.*

MATTHEW 11:28 (MSG)

Jesus taught that we should value people over tasks.
When you give as He gave—sharing your time with
others, caring for people, and offering comfort where
needed—you can experience life in an unhurried, calm,
and peaceful way. It's the perfect way to understand the
"unforced rhythms of grace."

*Heavenly Father, when I make the time to get away
with You, walk with You, and work with You, I experience the divine groove of stress-free, faith-filled living.*

Reflections

7

38

Sufficient in His Hands

"How many loaves do you have?" Jesus asked.
"Seven," they replied, "and a few small fish."

MATTHEW 15:34 (NIV)

———◆———

Jesus is at His best when the odds are at their worst. In
the above verse, Jesus faced a crowd of a thousand hungry people with seven loaves of bread and a few fish, but
amazingly it was more than enough. Instead of worrying about what you don't have, focus on abundance and
trust in Jesus's provision.

Heavenly Father, because of You I know
I will always have enough.

Reflections

Break Down Barriers
to Prayer

*I have tried hard to find you—don't let me
wander from your commands.*

PSALM 119:10 (NLT)

Sometimes we place roadblocks on our prayer journey.
We make excuses about being too busy, too tired, and
too distracted, but the truth is that all of these things
can be a springboard to prayer. Whatever is stopping
you from spending more time on your faith, reach out
to God and ask for His help.

*Heavenly Father, give me the grace to change
and help me to remember what an amazing gift
it is to spend time with You.*

Reflections

God Sees You!

She answered God by name, praying to the God who spoke to her, "You're the God who sees me! Yes! He saw me; and then I saw him!" That's how that desert spring got named "God-Alive-Sees-Me Spring." That spring is still there, between Kadesh and Bered.

GENESIS 16:13–16 (MSG)

———————◆———————

There are seasons in life when it may seem that no one understands or cares. God will show up in your time of need just as He did for Hagar. When you feel unseen, He reminds you that you are in His sights. During these times, Jesus gives us what we need most: Himself.

Heavenly Father, I know You see me!

Reflections

Failure Strengthens Faith

*But I have prayed for you that your faith may
not fail. And when you have turned again,
strengthen your brothers.*

LUKE 22:32 (ESV)

At the Last Supper, Jesus predicted that Peter's faith
would falter, that he would deny his relationship with
Him. But Jesus also knew that Peter would return to
Him. Peter's story teaches us that when we stumble on
our faith journey, it's not our fall that matters, but the
fact that we pick ourselves up and continue on His path.

*God of fair beginnings, no matter how badly things have
gone, You always make it possible for me to start again.*

Reflections

Victorious Forgetfulness

*Forgetting those things which are behind and
reaching forward to those things which are ahead,
I press toward the goal for the prize of the
upward call of God in Christ Jesus.*

PHILIPPIANS 3:13–14 (NKJV)

Norman Vincent Peale referred to "victorious forget-fulness" as the art of forgetting about the things holding you back, letting go, and reaching forward for what lies ahead. Yesterday is over. Focus on today.

Heavenly Father, thank You for Your great truth and all Your reminders that tomorrow will be wonderful. Help me forget the past and live today with a consciousness of the greatness and the opportunity of life.

Reflections

Time to Rest

Come to Me, all you *who labor and are heavy laden, and I will give you rest.*

MATTHEW 11:28 (NKJV)

Do you feel like you're too busy to rest? Are you always rushing from place to place when you're exhausted? No matter how packed your schedule is, you don't have time NOT to rest. Making time to nurture yourself is an important part of your faith. Resting helps you recharge and form a better relationship with God. When you are at your best, you can give your best back to the Lord.

Dear Lord, the next time I'm tired and struggling with my workload, I will say this verse aloud: "My Presence will go with you, *and I will give you rest"* (Exodus 33:14, NKJV).

Reflections

Begin Each Day
with Devotion

This is the day the LORD has made.
We will rejoice and be glad in it.

PSALM 118:24 (NLT)

W hen you arise, say the above verse out loud three times—but personalize it and say, "I will rejoice and be glad in it." Repeat it in a strong, clear voice and believe it! Decide to focus on the positive. Seek God's presence and ask Him to help you see opportunity instead of difficulty. Take His hand and ask Him to guide you to spend your day in ways that will bring glory to Him.

Heavenly Father, today is going to be a wonderful day! With Your help, I can successfully handle all problems that come my way.

Reflections

Learning to Recognize
Answers to Prayer

*Do not be anxious about anything, but in every
situation, by prayer and petition, with thanksgiving,
present your requests to God.*

PHILIPPIANS 4:6 (NIV)

Often we go from one concern to another without pausing to recognize that God regularly helps us
through our problems. What was worrying you a year
ago, a month ago? Take a moment to look back and
consider the obstacles you have overcome with God's
help.

*Heavenly Father, thank You for Your part in solving
my past problems and for standing by me today
when life seems overwhelming!*

Reflections

Who Am I?

He then asked, "And you—what are you saying about me? Who am I?" Peter gave the answer: "You are the Christ, the Messiah."

MARK 8:29 (MSG)

The true foundation of your life is answering this question about Jesus and recognizing how your answer shapes your relationship with Him. Every day your actions, your words, and your prayers reveal what you believe about His identity.

A prayer from Matthew 6:9 (NRSV): *"Pray then in this way: Our Father in heaven, hallowed be your name."*

Reflections

Be Happy Right Now

Be joyful always.

1 THESSALONIANS 5:16 (GNT)

The moment to be happy is now. Don't waste time thinking that happiness lies ahead—on the heels of a goal reached or making a big purchase. Take a moment and meditate on the goodness of God. Happiness is created with God's help, within yourself.

Heavenly Father, thank You for showing me that happiness flows through me when I focus on You and Your goodness.

Reflections

DAY
48

The Upside of Anger

*When I heard their outcry and
these charges, I was very angry.*

NEHEMIAH 5:6 (NIV)

Anger can be a good thing. It can help guide you out of situations that need changing and give you the impetus to make important decisions. So if you feel angry about something, instead of pushing it down deep, let it come to the surface and examine it. Use your feelings to uncover problems that need your attention.

*Dear Lord, help me learn from my anger
and then release it.*

Reflections

The Grace of Gratitude

*For it is by grace you have been saved, through faith—
and this is not from yourselves, it is the gift of God.*

EPHESIANS 2:8 (NIV)

Do you make the mistake of thinking that if everything isn't going your way, you can't possibly feel gratitude for the things that are? Gratitude is in and of itself a form of peace. When you recognize simple blessings, you open your heart to feel God's presence.

*Heavenly Father, thank You for the many blessings,
from sunrise to sunset, that grace my life!*

Reflections

A Psalm 91 Life

*If you say, "The LORD is my refuge," and you make the
Most High your dwelling, no harm will overtake you.*

PSALM 91:9–10 (NIV)

God is your refuge. He will deliver you from any difficulties, fears, and troubles, no matter how long they last. Though you may have difficulties, you will be able to handle all of them, for God will give His angels charge over you. His goodness and love will always surround you and will protect and guide you on the path of life.

*Heavenly Father, I will write this psalm on
my heart so that no matter how hard my life
may be, I will always be on top of things.*

Reflections

You Have Already Won

And it came to pass at the seventh time, when the priests blew with the trumpets, Joshua said unto the people, Shout; for the Lord hath given you the city.

JOSHUA 6:16 (KJV)

In the above verse, the Israelites were given instructions to march around the city blowing horns for days in order to win Jericho. Most likely, they were confused by the orders, and yet they obeyed and trusted Him. When you are up against defeat, express your faith, loudly. Even in the face of doubt and confusion, triumph will be yours.

Heavenly Father, when I face seemingly impossible obstacles, I will shout Your praises knowing that because of You, I have already won.

Reflections

Interruptions Happen

*Commit your way to the LORD; trust in him
and he will do this.*

PSALM 37:5 (NIV)

Sometimes distractions pull us away from our time with God. Best intentions for devotion can be detoured by a pressing need. Instead of getting upset, squeeze in time whenever you can. Commit your way to the Lord and trust that interruptions are part of His plan.

Heavenly Father, if a distraction needs my attention, be with me along the way and guide me back to You.

Reflections

Grow Through Difficulties

Look to the LORD and his strength; seek his face always.

1 CHRONICLES 16:11 (NIV)

Life's struggles make it possible to grow in strength and understanding. No matter what you face, Almighty God has placed within you the power to overcome overwhelming situations. Tap into the Source and face life's problems with God's help.

Dear Lord, because You are my strength in times of trouble, I know You are always there to help me.

Reflections

23.

DAY

54

Believing Is Beautiful

But if I say, "I will not mention his word or speak anymore in his name," his word is in my heart like a fire, a fire shut up in my bones. I am weary of holding it in; indeed, I cannot.

JEREMIAH 20:9 (NIV)

Beliefs aren't something we take lightly. When we believe in something, we feel it with passion and love. We defend and honor our beliefs. So when we accept Jesus Christ as our personal Savior and totally believe in Him, our lives are filled with new hope and new meaning. As in the above verse, the heat in your heart tells you of His inner presence. Your actions tell others.

Heavenly Father, may my life manifest Your love.

Reflections

The Lighter Side

*He will yet fill your mouth with laughter
and your lips with shouts of joy.*

JOB 8:21 (NIV)

Laughter and joy are great sources of strength. When
you choose to see the humor in a situation by looking to
the lighter side during dark times, you discover that you
can find joy even in the midst of trouble.

*Heavenly Father, You are the Light of the Lighter side. Fill
me with Your joy so that I smile easily and laugh out loud.*

Reflections

Three Blessings

Give thanks to the God of heaven.
His love endures forever.

PSALM 136:26 (NIV)

E. M. Bounds wrote, "Giving thanks is the very life of prayer. It is its fragrance and music, its poetry and its crown." Try this prayer technique: every day, thank God for three things—any three blessings that come to you. Praying gratefully is a key to seeing all that is right in your life.

Heavenly Father, thank You for blessing me with
Your Word, for giving me the wisdom to recognize
Your grace in my life and for this moment, right now,
when I feel Your love in my heart.

Reflections

Add You to Your To-Do List

*Or do you not know that your body is a temple
of the Holy Spirit within you, whom you have from
God? You are not your own, for you were bought
with a price. So glorify God in your body.*

1 CORINTHIANS 6:19–20 (ESV)

Do you make time to nurture yourself? When you neglect your own needs, the effects ripple down to all other aspects of your life. Every day spend at least ten minutes treating yourself, whether it be drinking a cup of tea, relaxing in a bath, or simply lying in bed just a few minutes longer each morning, looking forward to the blessings that will unfold in the day ahead.

Dear Lord, today I will schedule time for me and You.

Reflections

Respond with Love

But to you who are listening I say: Love your enemies, do good to those who hate you, bless those who curse you, pray for those who mistreat you.

LUKE 6:27–28 (NIV)

———◆———

Fighting fire with fire may work in forests, but it isn't effective when it comes to relationships. Jesus taught that we should bless those who curse us and return good for evil. It isn't productive to respond to anger with anger, or to hate with hate. As difficult as it may seem, Jesus promises peace to those who follow His instructions.

Restrain me, Lord. Help me draw upon Your peace and respond with love.

Reflections

Keep Away from Comparisons

Each one should test their own actions. Then they can take pride in themselves alone, without comparing themselves to someone else.

GALATIANS 6:4 (NIV)

Comparing yourself to others is destructive. You'll either feel discouraged or become arrogant. As Theodore Roosevelt said, "Comparison is the thief of joy." Instead of looking to others, focus on your purpose and be the person God made you to be.

Dear Lord, help me find satisfaction by doing my best and avoid the trap of comparing myself to others.

Reflections

Be Complete

The kingdom of God is within you.

LUKE 17:21 (KJV)

———————◆———————

God has placed all the abilities you need in your spirit. Believe in yourself, and the strength within you will surface. When you feel overwhelmed and weak, repeat these words: "God's abundance and power are within me. I lack for nothing."

Lord Jesus, may I abide in the peace of
Your kingdom now and forever.

Reflections

Your Alabaster Jar

*While he was in Bethany, reclining at the table
in the home of Simon the Leper, a woman came
with an alabaster jar of very expensive perfume,
made of pure nard. She broke the jar and
poured the perfume on his head.*

MARK 14:3 (NIV)

The woman with the alabaster jar understood what she
was doing when she poured very expensive perfume on
Jesus's head. There are times in life for us, too, to break
the alabaster jar—to spend lavishly and selflessly—to forget the expense and give from the heart.

*Jesus, may every demonstration of my love
honor You. How I would love for You to say
to me, as You did to the woman in Bethany,
"She has done a beautiful thing to me."*

Reflections

His Word in Your Heart

Thy word have I hid in mine heart that
I might not sin against thee.

PSALM 119:11 (KJV)

The psalmist who wrote the verse above believes the best place to keep God's Word is deep in the heart. In other words, know His instructions and memorize them so they are readily at hand, available to draw on when guidance is needed. Hide His Word in your heart and you'll have all the security you need.

Lord, help me infuse Your Word into my life.

Reflections

Wake Up to Jesus's Love

When I awake, I am still with thee.

PSALM 139:18 (KJV)

This scripture is the secret to having a wonderful day, every day. As soon as you emerge from sleep, say the words of verse above and then add, "I am with God. He has watched over me throughout the night and has brought me to this new day. He will watch over me and guide me all day long."

Heavenly Father, open my eyes to the blessings of today. Wake me up with excitement and hope for the dawning of a new day.

Reflections

Beyond Expectation

*Now to him who is able to do immeasurably
more than all we ask or imagine, according to
his power that is at work within us, to him be glory.*

EPHESIANS 3:20-21 (NIV)

Jesus often gives us more than we ask for or even imagine. Think of a time when He answered your prayer in ways that exceeded your expectations. When this happens, we get a glimpse of His infinite power. We learn to trust that His plan is best for our lives.

*Heavenly Father, You are able to go above and
beyond all that we ask. You work in ways that
I could never have imagined.*

Reflections

Think Good Thoughts

In conclusion, my friends, fill your minds with those things that are good and that deserve praise: things that are true, noble, right, pure, lovely, and honorable.

PHILIPPIANS 4:8 (GNT)

During long nights or stretches of gloomy days, the world can seem like a dark place. "Change your thoughts and you change your world," Norman Vincent Peale advised—much like Paul urges in the scripture above. Bring heavenly light into your life! Fill your mind with good thoughts.

Dear God, when I'm downcast, You have the power to turn my darkness into Light.

Reflections

Kind Words

*Being strengthened with all power, according to
his glorious might, for all endurance and
patience with joy.*

COLOSSIANS 1:11 (ESV)

How often do you tell the people in your life how much you appreciate them? God wants you to enlighten others with His joy by being kind and patient, and by showing others your appreciation and love. Make a list of your loved ones and make a commitment to let them know how much you care. When you tell someone how much they mean to you, you receive an unexpected boost of love and joy yourself!

*Dear God, thank You for giving me Your true
contentment and inspiring me to live generously.*

Reflections

Move Mountains

*Truly I tell you, if anyone says to this mountain,
"Go, throw yourself into the sea," and does not doubt
in their heart but believes that what they say will
happen, it will be done for them.*

MARK 11:23 (NIV)

Faith opens the door to miracles. Is a mountainous difficulty challenging you? Pray to God and ask him to help you move the mountain right now. Believe in His infinite power and don't doubt or underestimate what He can do.

*Heavenly Father, I believe You can move
mountains. I believe!*

Reflections

Faith for Rainy Days

*Do you know how God controls the storm and
causes the lightning to flash from his clouds?*

JOB 37:15 (NLT)

It's easy to see God's goodness when the sun is shining and all is well, but His goodness is also present on cloudy, rainy days. Every type of weather serves a purpose, and every day meets our needs. So if you face a gray day, or if you're entering a season of bleak weather in the region where you live, have faith and know in your heart that God's plan is at work.

*Dear Lord, I am receptive to Your ways in the
sunshine of life and in the rainy days.*

Reflections

Rainbow Blessings

*Whenever the rainbow appears in the clouds,
I will see it and remember the everlasting
covenant between God and all living
creatures of every kind on the earth.*

GENESIS 9:16 (NIV)

Many times throughout the Bible, God creates visible signs to help people remember His promises. The rainbow is a breathtaking symbol of God's blessing and a stunning reminder of the triumph of mercy and the victory of grace. What blessed signs has God given you?

*Heavenly Father, thank You for the many reminders
You send to show me I am blessed.*

Reflections

DAY
70

The Power of Humility

*All of you, clothe yourselves with
humility toward one another.*

1 PETER 5:5 (NIV)

The Bible makes it clear that a humble heart is essential
to spiritual growth. How do we aim for humility? One
answer lies in Paul's letter to the Philippians where
he suggests, "In your relationships with one another,
have the same mindset as Christ Jesus" (Philippians 2:5).

*Heavenly Father, I will follow Your example
and clothe myself in humility.*

Reflections

God's Will Power

*For this very reason, make every effort to add to
your faith goodness; and to goodness, knowledge;
and to knowledge, self-control; and to self-control,
perseverance; and to perseverance, godliness.*

2 PETER 1:5–6 (NIV)

Little things can test your self-control, whether it's
a decadent dessert that threatens your diet or over-
spending for some special occasion. A large part of self-
control is about willpower or, more specifically, "God's
will" power. By focusing on Him and asking for His help
and strength, you can stand firm when you feel tempted.

*Lead me today, Lord. Help me have the discipline
to follow Your will and turn away from temptation.*

Reflections

Be Bold in Service

*Bear one another's burdens, and so fulfill
the law of Christ.*

GALATIANS 6:2 (NKJV)

Do you feel overwhelmed by what is going on today—
the problems that so many face, whether it's in your
own family, your neighborhood, or the world? Ask God
to show you where you are needed most. Make a list of
places where you can volunteer and pray for guidance
on where to help.

*Heavenly Father, make me bold in service for You.
Direct me to do Your good works.*

Reflections

Shine Your Light from Within

When Jesus spoke again to the people, he said, "I am the light of the world. Whoever follows me will never walk in darkness, but will have the light of life."

JOHN 8:12 (NIV)

Elisabeth Kübler-Ross said, "People are like stained-glass windows. They sparkle and shine when the sun is out, but when the darkness sets in, their true beauty is revealed only if there is a light from within." Do you hold the Light of Christ in your heart? When you reflect His love, compassion, and wisdom into the world, you glow with His beauty.

Heavenly Father, radiate Your loving Light through me. Transform me by the glow of Your Spirit; the deeper the darkness, the brighter I will shine.

Reflections

Be Made Well

If I only touch his cloak, I will be healed.

MATTHEW 9:21 (NIV)

The Lord has tremendous curative power. When you are in need of His healing, all you need to do is extend your hand and reach out in faith. Know that you are safe. He will enfold you in His loving arms. He will comfort and heal you.

Heavenly Father, thank You for rescuing me—for making me well.

Reflections

One Grateful Leper

*Jesus asked, "Were not all ten cleansed?
Where are the other nine?"*

LUKE 17:17 (NIV)

I n the above scripture, Jesus healed ten lepers but only one threw himself at Jesus's feet and thanked Him. Gratitude is an important part of faith—a spiritual discipline that opens our hearts to His love. What are you thankful for? Share your praise with Him.

*Heavenly Father, thank You for the gifts that
you give me each and every day—especially the ones
I have forgotten to be grateful for!*

Reflections

A Comforting Prayer

He heals the brokenhearted and binds up their wounds.

PSALM 147:3 (NIV)

Turn to this verse when you are feeling brokenhearted from loss or sorrow. Trust that God is helping you heal. Know that mourning comes in many different stages, so be patient and understanding with yourself. Believe that tomorrow will be better. Find special comfort in praying the Psalms.

Heavenly Father, envelop me in Your tender care.
Wrap Your arms around me and hold me tight.
Send Your comfort now.

Reflections

Clean Your Spirit

*Cleanse me with hyssop, and I will be clean;
wash me, and I will be whiter than snow.*

PSALM 51:7 (NIV)

Ask God for guidance as you dig deep into the clutter and grime of your spiritual life. Purge negative feelings and thoughts. Release resentments and forgive any wrongdoings. Break any bad habits. Go through your life and see what's getting in the way of your relationship with God.

*Heavenly Father, clean every nook and
cranny of my heart and spirit. Wash me clean
by Your Spirit and Your Word.*

Reflections

Stay on the Holy Highway

*And a highway will be there; it will be called the
Way of Holiness; it will be for those who walk on
that Way. The unclean will not journey on it;
wicked fools will not go about on it.*

ISAIAH 35:8 (NIV)

Y ou are progressing on the Way of Holiness. Reflect on
how you feel as you move toward being more fully centered
on God's will. Take a moment and praise God for the
positive changes happening in your faith and your life.

*Lord, keep me moving forward spiritually.
Help me keep on the path to holiness.*

Reflections

Don't Plead...Please!

*For God is working in you, giving you the desire
and the power to do what pleases him.*

PHILIPPIANS 2:13 (NLT)

When you pray, do you plead for what you want and
try to convince God that you know best? Instead pray
this verse. Let Scripture move your spirit more closely to
His will rather than fighting for your own way. Center
your heart on pleasing God.

*Lord, I need Your help in letting go of what I want.
Help me to focus my effort on pleasing You instead.*

Reflections

A Man After God's Own Heart

I have found David the son of Jesse, a man after mine own heart, which shall fulfill all my will.

ACTS 13:22 (KJV)

Despite King David's flaws, he is described in the Bible as a man after God's own heart. Although David was not perfect, his mind, will, and soul were in accord with God. David serves as an example of how to live a humble, respectful, faithful, obedient, and devoted life.

Merciful God, though my actions and thoughts may not always be perfect, I long for You to say, "You are truly after my own heart!"

Reflections

Move Beyond the Problem

*Jesus stopped and called them. "What do you
want me to do for you?" he asked. "Lord," they
answered, "we want our sight."*

MATTHEW 20:32–33 (NIV)

Is there an aspect of your life where you feel stuck?
Maybe it's a job where you've stayed too long, or a project that you just can't seem to get done. Pray. Ask God
to open your eyes to see new solutions.

*Heavenly Father, I can't move forward. Help guide
me to new ideas and the energy to follow through.*

Reflections

Stand Firm
Against Temptation

*Your commands are always with me and
make me wiser than my enemies.*

PSALM 119:98 (NIV)

Memorizing scripture is a helpful way to fight temptation. When you know God's Word and can apply it to your life, you are better able to protect your heart, your spirit, and your values. By committing yourself to the goal of reading the Bible consistently, you can surrender your personal wants for His will.

*Heavenly Father, help me to put Your Word
first in every decision I make and prayerfully
move forward, trusting You to guide me as I go.*

Reflections

Shine the Light
of Gratitude

*Praise the LORD. Give thanks to the LORD,
for he is good; his love endures forever.*

PSALM 106:1 (NIV)

Norman Vincent Peale said that when we give thanks, we not only recognize past blessings—we activate blessings to come. All of us have simple, beautiful things that the Almighty God has given us, which we can appreciate. Open your eyes and see that God does "wonderful things without number" (Job 5:9, CEB) every day! Praise Him for the good in your life.

*Dear Lord, thank You for the bounty
of blessings You have given me.*

Reflections

DAY
84

When Things Fall Apart

Be content with what you have, because God has said,
"Never will I leave you; never will I forsake you."

HEBREWS 13:5 (NIV)

The word "contentment" derives from two Latin words, *con* and *tenere*, meaning "to hold together." When you have faith in God, your mind will "hold together" so efficiently that you can recover from any disappointment or crisis. If you always remember that God is on your side, you can be content no matter what comes your way.

Heavenly Father, I can live a life of contentment, even when things seem to fall apart, because I know You are holding all things together.

Reflections

Value Your Soul

*I will make them and the places surrounding
my hill a blessing. I will send down showers
in season; there will be showers of blessing.*

EZEKIEL 34:26 (NIV)

Reflect on the beautiful words of Teresa of Avila: "Each of us has a soul, but we forget to value it. We don't remember that we are creatures made in the image of God. We don't understand the great secrets hidden inside of us." The Lord is generous—He showers His abundance on your life.

*Heavenly Father, I am filled with gratitude
for Your many blessings.*

Reflections

Preventative Spiritual Care

My child, pay attention to what I say. Listen carefully to my words. Don't lose sight of them. Let them penetrate deep into your heart, for they bring life to those who find them, and healing to their whole body.

PROVERBS 4:20–22 (NLT)

Check in on your faith life. Are you praying every day, not just when crisis strikes or you have a problem to solve? Develop a deep connection with God and keep Him informed of your fears and worries; ask Him for solutions before your problems escalate. As the saying goes, an ounce of prevention is worth a pound of cure.

Heavenly Father, I don't know what the future holds, but I find comfort in knowing that You hold the future.

Reflections

God Is Guiding Your Path

*For he will order his angels to protect
you wherever you go.*

PSALM 91:11 NLT

Nothing in this world can hurt you! God is making
sure you stay safe, wherever you go. His amazing kindness surrounds and guides you. You can go through
life with a contented spirit, knowing God watches over
you—no matter what comes your way.

*Thank You, Father. I know that no matter how
alone or lost I feel, You know where I am and
are able to guide me to follow Your direction.*

Reflections

Reframe Your Perspective

You, therefore, have no excuse, you who pass judgment on someone else, for at whatever point you judge another, you are condemning yourself, because you who pass judgment do the same things.

ROMANS 2:1 (NIV)

———

Take this verse to heart and make an effort to stop judging others. If you find yourself thinking unkind thoughts, reframe your perspective from a lens of compassion and understanding. Say a prayer for wisdom and help to stop being so critical of others. Instead, focus on being helpful.

Understanding Father, sometimes I judge those around me. Help me to love them instead, to make them feel accepted and comforted. May I welcome them into my heart.

Reflections

Set Your Spirit for More Light

As long as I am in the world, I am the light of the world.

JOHN 9:5 (ESV)

The word *light* appears more than two hundred times in the Bible. Light represents the presence of God. Light gives us comfort and understanding. We strive to walk in God's light. Today, as you encounter light in its many forms, consider the importance of light in your spiritual life.

Lord, today I will concentrate on letting in more of Your glorious light.

Reflections

Abound in Hope

*May the God of hope fill you with all joy
and peace in believing, so that by the power
of the Holy Spirit you may abound in hope.*

ROMANS 15:13 (ESV)

———

W hat's the condition of hope in your life at this very moment? Does it get up with you every morning? Does it carry you confidently through the day? Is it still there, sustaining you, as you fall asleep? If cares, worries, fears, and discouragement have gained ascendancy in your mind, then open the windows of your soul and let a strong, fresh current of hope come surging through!

*Heavenly Father, fill my spirit with hope. Replace
any negativity I have with energy, confidence, and
enthusiasm for what You are doing in my life.*

Reflections

God in the Rearview Mirror

For You have been my help, and in the shadow of Your wings I sing for joy.

PSALM 63:7 (NASB)

———————————•———————————

When you feel lost and uncertain about what the future holds, pause for a moment and look back at your life. Reflect on the many instances where you were guided and blessed by God; the times when you could clearly feel Him helping you. Know He is with you now. He is helping you.

Merciful God, when I am in the midst of a difficult time and cannot recognize Your presence in my life, I trust You are helping me. I know I am not alone.

Reflections

Release Your Fears to God

*So do not fear, for I am with you; do not be dismayed,
for I am your God. I will strengthen you and help you;
I will uphold you with my righteous right hand.*

ISAIAH 41:10 (NIV)

What are you afraid of? Whether it's dread of loneliness, loss, catastrophe, or suffering, all of us have something that triggers anxiety and separates us from God. Share your worries with the Lord and ask Him to transform your weakness into strength.

*Heavenly Father, release the fear that is
wrapped around my heart. Transform
my worry into courage. Make me brave.*

Reflections

Know When to Say No

*For God gave us a spirit not of fear but
of power and love and self-control.*

2 TIMOTHY 1:7 (ESV)

Knowing when to say no or when to ask for help is an important part of life. When your cup runneth over, perhaps it's time to say no or to look for ways you might downsize your responsibilities. When you empty your cup of the things you cannot hold, you make room for new blessings.

Great and awesome God, help me find rest when I'm stressed. Give me the courage to say no and to ask for help. Remind me that the best use of my time is serving You.

Reflections

Soar with the Eagles

*But those who hope in the L*ORD *will renew their strength. They will soar on wings like eagles; they will run and not grow weary, they will walk and not be faint.*

ISAIAH 40:31 (NIV)

This beautiful verse describes the greatest experience that can ever happen to you—spiritual renewal. By completely surrendering yourself to God and putting your faith in Him, you will feel God's strength guiding you and giving you energy.

Dear Lord, renew my spirit so that I rise above life's challenges and soar like the eagles.

Reflections

A Purpose Behind
Every Problem

*Let your roots grow down into Christ and draw up
nourishment from him. See that you go on growing in
the Lord, and become strong and vigorous in the truth.*

COLOSSIANS 2:7 (TLB)

God wants you to grow in character. When you dedicate your life to becoming like Him, you understand that everything that happens to you has spiritual significance. There is a purpose behind every problem.

*Heavenly Father, thank You for using life's trials
to help us grow to be better people.*

Reflections

A Good Friend in Time of Crisis

When Job's three friends . . . heard about all the troubles that had come upon him, they set out from their homes and met together by agreement to go and sympathize with him and comfort him.

JOB 2:11 (NIV)

Do you ever find yourself not knowing what to say? Perhaps a friend tells you that she is terribly depressed, or someone is deeply grieving over the loss of a loved one. If this happens, pray for God to give you the right words to say. If that doesn't help, just sit with her and let her know you'll hold her in your thoughts and prayers.

Heavenly Father, help me be a source of comfort to my friends. Guide my words and actions by Your pure love.

Reflections

God Is Your Refuge

God is our refuge and strength,
a very present help in trouble.

PSALM 46:1 (KJV)

When you feel overwhelmed and burdened by your responsibilities, take this verse to heart. Don't try to handle everything by yourself. God is your protection, your solace, your comfort, and your refuge. Let Him flow in. Loosen your grip on the idea that you have to control everything, and put the future into the hands of God.

Heavenly Father, I know that You are my refuge,
my strength, and my very present help.
I open my heart and invite You in.

Reflections

Peace from God's Word

*Let the peace of Christ rule in your hearts,
since as members of one body you were
called to peace. And be thankful.*

COLOSSIANS 3:15 (NIV)

To relax your spirit, fill your mind with God's Word. "Come to me, all you who are weary and burdened, and I will give you rest" (Matthew 11:28, NIV). "Peace I leave with you; my peace I give you. I do not give to you as the world gives. Do not let your hearts be troubled and do not be afraid" (John 14:27, NIV). Let these verses sink deeply into your mind and spirit.

*Heavenly Father, shine Your radiance on
all aspects of my life. Your Word is balm for
my soul, a blessed oasis of rest and renewal.*

Reflections

Your Walk with God

*The next day Jesus decided to leave for Galilee.
Finding Philip, he said to him, "Follow me."*

JOHN 1:43 (NIV)

———————✦———————

Jesus guided His disciples not only with His words, but
with His walk. He modeled how to share the good news,
how to live a life of prayer, and so much more. You are
also an example to others. The road you travel with Christ
isn't just for you, but for all those who follow and learn.

*Help me, Jesus, to focus on Your ways.
Help me to walk by Your truth.*

Reflections

When You Are Afraid

There is no fear in love. But perfect love drives out
fear, because fear has to do with punishment.
The one who fears is not made perfect in love.

1 JOHN 4:18 (NIV)

———

The Bible tells us specifically, "Do not fear" (Isaiah 41:10, NIV). But since we're not perfect, for most of us, fear is a part of life. When you feel afraid, fight fear with faith. Let petitions and praises shape your worries into prayers.

Lord, thank You for being with me. I know
You can turn the worst into the best. You are
bigger than anything I fear.

Reflections

God's Good Work

*For we are God's handiwork, created in
Christ Jesus to do good works, which God
prepared in advance for us to do.*

EPHESIANS 2:10 (NIV)

T oday, thank God for working in your life. He is constantly preparing you for moments and situations that
are uniquely yours. By praying and engaging in His
Word, you have welcomed Him into your life. Rejoice!
You are an instrument of His grace.

*Dear Lord, thank You for the good work
You have prepared for me. When I trust
Your plan, miracles happen.*

Reflections

Tune in to God's Voice

*While you were doing all these things, declares
the LORD, I spoke to you again and again, but you
did not listen; I called you, but you did not answer.*

JEREMIAH 7:13 (NIV)

Is something distracting you from hearing God's voice? Are you creating the time and focus to recognize His guidance? Your Heavenly Father sends His words of wisdom and peace again and again. Quiet your mind to receive His messages.

*Dear Lord, I seek Your voice and long to hear
Your promises and plans for me.*

Reflections

Infinite Possibilities

*When I consider your heavens, the work of your
fingers, the moon and the stars, which you have set in
place, what is mankind that you are mindful of them,
human beings that you care for them?*

PSALM 8:3–4 (NIV)

W hen you go outside at night and gaze upward at the
heavens, take in the vast beauty of the moon and stars.
Recognize the infinite possibilities of God's work. Apply
that awesome and fresh point of view to your own situation and what you perceive as your problems.

*Dear Lord, when I am focused on my problems,
and most likely making mountains out of molehills,
guide me to go outside, look upward, and have
faith in Your omnipotence.*

Reflections

Stones of Remembrance

*Choose twelve men from among the people, one
from each tribe, and tell them to take up twelve
stones ... These stones are to be a memorial
to the people of Israel forever.*

JOSHUA 4:2–3, 7 (NIV)

When you look back at your life, do you focus on the successes, celebrations, and victories? Remember the amazing moments of God's work in your life. These "stones of remembrance" help you overcome stumbling blocks and weather life's storms.

Heavenly Father, thank You for the many ways You help me. I will remember them deep in my heart and turn to them when I need hope and reassurance of Your glory.

Reflections

When Your Prayers Run Dry

You will seek me and find me when you seek me with all your heart.

JEREMIAH 29:13 (NIV)

Everyone experiences a dry period in their faith—a time when they feel uninspired and unheard in prayer. It's important to realize that everyone has them, and the way out…is to pray anyway. Reach out to God and ask Him to heal the deserts in your spiritual life.

Lord, together we can work for Your glory.

Reflections

Secret to Success

*In all your ways submit to him, and
he will make your paths straight.*

PROVERBS 3:6 (NIV)

Are you ready to experience abundance? Look ahead and let go of any fear of the future. Do everything you can to achieve your goal, and then turn the situation over to God. Completely believe in His power to help you. Have faith that you will be successful.

*Heavenly Father, I know You have a wonderful
plan for my life. Please help me to live a blessed
life of purpose and perseverance.*

Reflections

Be Free!

So if the Son sets you free, you will be free indeed.

JOHN 8:36 (NIV)

Jesus came so that we could have life and have it more abundantly. As the above verse promises, when Christ sets you free, "you will be free indeed" and live a life of grace, free from fear. Rejoice, and let Him take away your worries and burdens!

A prayer from Psalm 56:3–4: *When I am afraid, I put my trust in you. In God, whose word I praise—in God I trust and am not afraid. What can mere mortals do to me?*

Reflections

Silver Linings

These [trials] have come so that the proven genuineness of your faith—of greater worth than gold, which perishes even though refined by fire—may result in praise, glory and honor when Jesus Christ is revealed.

1 PETER 1:7 (NIV)

There is no doubt about it: pain and suffering immediately put life in perspective. When we are grieving or in pain, all that seemed important before falls away, and we are left with the core of what matters most. Our surrender to the moment—surrender to what we feel—is an opportunity for personal growth. The silver lining of our struggles is that they help us become more compassionate, patient, and understanding people.

Keep me close to You, Lord. Replace my sorrow with the warmth of Your comfort.

Reflections

Allow Jesus to Guide You

The minute I said, "I'm slipping, I'm falling,"
your love, GOD, took hold and held me fast.
When I was upset and beside myself, you calmed
me down and cheered me up.

PSALM 94:18–19 (MSG)

When worry enters your mind, do you tense up and shut down? Sometimes fear about what will happen can be overwhelming. Instead of taking on a problem by yourself, take a deep breath and remember that God is in control. Invite Him to direct your life and ask Him to help you surrender to His guidance.

Heavenly Father, please help me truly trust
and allow You to guide my life.

Reflections

Great Morning Exercise

*Above all else, guard your heart, for
everything you do flows from it.*

PROVERBS 4:23 (NIV)

———————

Every morning, dedicate five minutes in silence to keep your heart in tune with God. Take in a deep breath and pray. Affirm that God is filling you with strength and energy. Feel His love and power fill your spirit.

*Magnificent Creator God, help me to keep my mind,
body, and spirit in tune with You so that I can be
a vessel for Your good works.*

Reflections

The Widow's Offering

*All these people gave their gifts out of their wealth; but
she out of her poverty put in all she had to live on.*

LUKE 21:4 (NIV)

Jesus's story in this scripture is one of the greatest
sermons on giving that has ever been preached. The
Bible tells us that if you give "out of poverty," you will
receive great blessings. Why not put this principle in
practice today? Be prepared to receive an outpouring
of God's unfathomable love.

*Lord, help me remember that You have given me
far more than I can ever give in return.*

Reflections

Big Faith, Big Life

Everything is possible for one who believes.

MARK 9:23 (NIV)

Norman Vincent Peale said that how you live your life is directly proportional to how greatly you believe. Believe little and you will have a little life. If your belief is weak, you will get a weak life. If your faith is fear-based, you will live a life of fear. But when you believe big, you get a big life!

*Heavenly Father, God of possibilities, I believe
Your plans surpass my biggest dreams.*

Reflections

Build on the Cornerstone

The stone the builders rejected has become the cornerstone.

PSALM 118:22 (NIV)

In the above verse, Jesus is "the stone the builders rejected," and yet he became the cornerstone of faith. He served with peace and love—with dignity—strengthening the very structure of our belief system, despite having been rejected.

Dear Lord, when I am faced with rejection, help me to continue and respond with a loving heart.

Reflections

Where Are You Going?

*The angel said to her, "Hagar, Sarai's servant, where
have you come from, and where are you going?" "I'm
running away from my mistress, Sarai," she replied.*

GENESIS 16:8 (NLT)

Despite careful planning, sometimes circumstances
force you into a situation where your options aren't
what you want. Like Hagar in the above verse, there are
times where you have to go back to a place you didn't
want to, or surrender to a situation that you hoped was
over. In those times, it's best to take a deep breath and
accept God's will.

*Lord, I trust Your plan and Your path.
Your will, not mine.*

Reflections

Is Your Truth
God's Truth?

*Guide me in your truth and teach me, for you are
God my Savior, and my hope is in you all day long.*

PSALM 25:5 (NIV)

Are you living a life of truth? Perhaps you are making excuses about something dishonest that you did, or you have been less than honest with yourself and others about a situation. If anything comes to mind, repeat the above verse. Allow the truth of His Word to enter into your mind, body, and soul. Feel the relief of the truth that sets you free.

*Lord, when I diligently seek You with all
my heart, You guide me in Your truth.*

Reflections

Keep Facing Forward

*I press on toward the goal to win the prize for which
God has called me heavenward in Christ Jesus.*

PHILIPPIANS 3:14 (NIV)

Being disappointed or hurt by a friend or loved one
sometimes happens. The good news is that you can control how you react. Instead of filling your life and time
with thoughts that sap your energy with regret and bitterness, fill them with light. Spend time with God. Ask
Him to help heal your broken heart.

*Heavenly Father, free me from past hurts and
heartbreak. Keep me facing forward. Guide me
to see the good in people. Help me heal.*

Reflections

Be "Full of God"

The zeal of the Lord Almighty will accomplish this.

ISAIAH 9:7 (NIV)

The word *enthusiasm* is based on the Greek word *enthou-siazein,* derived from *theos,* the Greek word for God. So "enthusiasm" literally means "full of God" or "inspired by God." God will help you maintain enthusiasm. He will help you overcome all difficulties, all tragedies, all sorrows, all heartaches; He will give you victory.

Dear Lord, help me let go of negativity so that I can walk this journey in ease and peace, enthusiastically— and live a life full of You.

Reflections

Balm for What-If Worries

Therefore do not worry about tomorrow,
for tomorrow will worry about itself. Each day
has enough trouble of its own.

MATTHEW 6:34 (NIV)

Often our biggest worries hinge on what is going to happen. Fear of the future can block us from the blessings of right now. The next time you find yourself preoccupied with what-if worries, remind yourself of the above scripture and believe that He has tomorrow covered. Stay hopeful in the present! It's the best thing you can do for your future.

Heavenly Father, thank You for this moment.
Thank You for today.

Reflections

Best Friends with God

*For since our friendship with God was restored by the
death of his Son while we were still his enemies, we will
certainly be saved through the life of his Son.*

ROMANS 5:10 (NLT)

You become close to God through constant conversation. Keep devotion time every day. Do your best to involve Him in every activity. You don't need to "get away" to spend time with God. Instead, get in the habit of praying throughout the day. Honor His presence.

*Heavenly Father, I want a deeper,
more intimate relationship with You.*

Reflections

Live God's Way

*But what happens when we live God's way? He
brings gifts into our lives, much the same way that
fruit appears in an orchard—things like affection
for others, exuberance about life, serenity. We
develop a willingness to stick with things, a sense
of compassion in the heart, and a conviction that a
basic holiness permeates things and people.*

GALATIANS 5:22 (MSG)

When you live God's way, He plants and cultivates fruit
in your life. Beautiful blessings—inspiration, endurance,
empathy, serenity—will grace your days. And God's love
will flow through you and onto others easily and naturally.

*Heavenly Father, help me remove habits or thoughts
that prevent me from living Your way.*

Reflections

A Call to Action

Get up! Pick up your mat and walk.

JOHN 5:8 (NIV)

Whﬞat is holding you back from living your best life? Is it fear, or focusing your attention on a situation or goal that you falsely believe holds the key to happiness? This uplifting verse is a call to action to cast away whatever hindrances are keeping you from God's blessing. Pick up your mat and rise to a new life, a new way of being and seeing.

Heavenly Father, I rise to Your call. Nothing can stop me. I am ready to live my best life.

Reflections

Forgive, Forgive, Forgive

*Then Peter came to Jesus and asked, "Lord, how
many times shall I forgive my brother or sister who
sins against me? Up to seven times?" Jesus answered,
"I tell you, not seven times, but seventy-seven times."*

MATTHEW 18:21–22 (NIV)

Jesus invites us to be like Him—to love the people in our
lives in spite of their wrongdoings and their shortcomings. He asks us to follow His teaching in the above verse
to forgive and forgive again, remembering that His forgiveness is limitless.

*Lord, it's not always easy to forgive. Heal my wounded
heart and teach me to love unconditionally.*

Reflections

Be a God Pleaser

*On the contrary, we speak as those approved by God
to be entrusted with the gospel. We are not trying to
please people but God, who tests our hearts.*

1 THESSALONIANS 2:4 (NIV)

Do you base your decisions on the goal of making other people happy? Try instead to focus on pleasing God first. If you're feeling torn and stretched in different directions, spend some quiet time asking Him to guide you and give you the courage to please Him.

Heavenly Father, I aim to please You always.

Reflections

Grace Upon Grace

From his fullness we have all received, grace upon grace.

JOHN 1:16 (ESV)

God showers you in a never-ending, constant supply of "grace upon grace." His blessings and favor flow over you, cleansing and satisfying you. If you feel unworthy or lacking, repeat the above verse and imagine His grace flowing upon you and filling you with divine light.

Heavenly Father, each day is a sacred gift, designed by You and filled with grace upon grace.

Reflections

When You Can't Pray

My prayer is not for them alone. I pray also for those who will believe in me through their message.

JOHN 17:20 (NIV)

Sometimes the most heartfelt prayers are the ones without words. In times when you feel unable to pray, know that Christ is praying for you. With both Jesus and the Holy Spirit, you are covered in prayer—even when you can't muster the strength or focus to pray yourself.

Lord Jesus, it is comforting to know that when I am too weak, the Mightiest keeps praying on my behalf.

Reflections

Just for Today

*So do not worry, saying, "What shall we eat?" or
"What shall we drink?" or "What shall we wear?"*

MATTHEW 6:31 (NIV)

I t's easy to get worked up about what might happen in
the future: Will I have enough money to pay my bills?
Will I become ill? Yet all you need to do is ask for what
you need today. As Jesus pointed out in Matthew, "Your
Father knows what you need before you ask him" (Matthew 6:8, NIV). Trust God with your needs today, this
day. That is enough.

*Heavenly Father, help me face the future with courage,
knowing that You have my needs covered today.*

Reflections

Pray Through Doubt

But the one who hears my words and does not put them into practice is like a man who built a house on the ground without a foundation.

LUKE 6:49 (NIV)

Do you sometimes feel your faith rests on shaky ground? Maybe you have suffered difficult blows like financial problems, the end of a relationship, or the loss of a loved one. When life fills you with doubt, turn to God's Word. Let His teachings strengthen your character so that the storms of life cannot break the steady foundation of your faith.

Dear Lord, thank You for giving me the strength to withstand difficulties—not the worse for wear, but better for the experience.

Reflections

A Hug from God

*And I pray that you, being rooted and established in
love, may have power, together with all the Lord's
holy people, to grasp how wide and long and high
and deep is the love of Christ, and to know this love
that surpasses knowledge—that you may be filled to
the measure of all fullness of God.*

EPHESIANS 3:17–19 (NIV)

God loves you unconditionally, no strings attached. He
loves you for who you are, right this very moment. He loves
you on good days and bad days. He may not love all the
things you do, but He always loves *you*—no matter what!

*I know You love me, Father. Thank You for
telling me every day in so many ways.*

Reflections

Grudge, Be Gone

Get rid of all bitterness, rage and anger, brawling and slander, along with every form of malice. Be kind and compassionate to one another, forgiving each other, just as in Christ God forgave you.

EPHESIANS 4:31–32 (NIV)

If you are having trouble forgiving someone, ask God today for the resources to soften your heart. Like a heavy stone lifted from around your neck, you will be free of a great weight, and you will be able to go forward unburdened by self-consuming resentment.

*Remind me, Father, how self-defeating
it is to hold grudges.*

Reflections

Praying in Secret

*But when you pray, go into your room, close the door
and pray to your Father, who is unseen. Then your
Father, who sees what is done in secret, will reward you.*

MATTHEW 6:6 (NIV)

This verse invites you to find a place where no one even
knows you are praying, shut the door, and talk to God
in secret. There is spiritual power in intimate prayer—in
sharing deep thoughts and emotions. Keep your words
between you and God and enter into an adventure that
is uniquely yours.

*Heavenly Father, thank You for being
my trusted friend. I long to know You better.*

Reflections

God Loves the Underdog

*Then the LORD raised up judges, who saved
them out of the hands of these raiders.*

JUDGES 2:16 (NIV)

Philip Yancey said, "Though the world may be tilted toward the rich and powerful, God is tilted toward the underdog." The Bible is filled with unlikely heroes, ordinary people that the world considered underdogs. When you think that a goal is out of reach and the odds are stacked against you, look to the Bible and the many examples of everyday people living lives of heroic faith.

*Dear Lord, when I feel discouraged, give me
a boost of Your confidence. Help me to remember
that because of You I will be victorious.*

Reflections

Who Are You Becoming?

And we know that in all things God works for the good of those who love him, who have been called according to his purpose.

ROMANS 8:28 (NIV)

Do you know who you want to be? Perhaps you haven't asked yourself that question since you were a child. The fact remains, the person you are and the person you are becoming is developed by the simple choices you make every day. Take a moment and reflect on who you want to become.

Heavenly Father, help me grow into the person I am here to become.

Reflections

Healing Promises

*For I will restore health to you, and your wounds
I will heal, declares the* LORD.

JEREMIAH 30:17 (ESV)

If you or someone you love is facing emotional or physical pain, turn to God in prayer. Fill your mind with the
healing power of His Word. Read and reread healing
scriptures such as Psalm 30:2, Psalm 103:3, and Jeremiah
30:17. Quiet your mind as you focus on God's restorative
power, welcoming His Word to your body and spirit.

*Great Physician, even when I'm not feeling my best,
I can be grateful for Your care. I commit myself
to Your loving arms.*

Reflections

Melt Stress Away

When anxiety was great within me,
your consolation brought me joy.

PSALM 94:19 (NIV)

When stress overpowers you, turn to God. If you feel burdened by taking on too much, recognize that it's not your job to make everything happen. Do what you can and trust that God will do His part. No matter what you are facing, look up and know that God will bring you joy.

Heavenly Father, thank You for relieving
my stress. Because of You I can handle any
and all of life's challenges.

Reflections

The Perfect Ending
to Every Day

Shout aloud and sing for joy, people of Zion,
for great is the Holy One of Israel among you.

ISAIAH 12:6 (NIV)

One way to develop inner joy in your life is to end your nights with prayers of gratitude. Each night, right before you go to sleep, instead of rehashing the day or worrying about tomorrow, count your blessings and thank God for every one of them. List everything that makes you happy, from the comfort of your home to the beauty of the clear blue sky. Pray these precious moments before sleep, connecting with God and the good in your life.

Heavenly Father, You are my joy! Thank You
for the countless ways You bless me.

Reflections

Your Life's Purpose

*We have different gifts, according to the
grace given to each of us.*

ROMANS 12:6 (NIV)

———————◆———————

Each one of us is put here on earth to make a difference. As Norman Vincent Peale said, "The best thing you have to give is yourself." Each day plant seeds of love, nurture those around you, find joy in everything you do, and never forget how important your life's work truly is.

Heavenly Father, on days when I lose sight of my purpose for being here, help me remember I'm doing this for You.

Reflections

Abiding and Bearing Fruit

*If you remain in me and my words remain in you,
ask whatever you wish, and it will be done for you.*

JOHN 15:7 (NIV)

Prayer is a fundamental step in knowing God. By taking His Word into your heart, you align your will with His. When your decisions and goals are backed by His power, your life will bear abundant fruit for His glory.

Lord, I abide in You.

Reflections

Embrace Change

For the Spirit God gave us does not make us timid,
but gives us power, love and self-discipline.

2 TIMOTHY 1:7 (NIV)

Change. The word itself can trigger anxiety. Fear of change can cause people to stay in unhealthy relationships, or continue to work where they are unhappy and have dismal futures. If you know something needs to change in your life—have courage. Use this verse as an affirmation to help you take a leap of faith. You are not alone. Blessings lie ahead.

Dear God, help me face the changes I should
make in my life; grant me the courage to leap.

Reflections

Food for Thought

*Finally, brothers, whatever is true, whatever is
honorable, whatever is just, whatever is pure,
whatever is lovely, whatever is commendable, if
there is any excellence, if there is anything worthy
of praise, think about these things.*

PHILIPPIANS 4:8 (ESV)

Sometimes negativity invades our thoughts and
plagues our lives, dragging us down. Philippians 4:8
advises us to guard our minds by fixing our thoughts on
Jesus. The best way to fill your head with good, healthy
thoughts is to concentrate on Him.

*Heavenly Father, clear my mind of unhappy thoughts.
Help me focus on You.*

Reflections

Run with Jesus

Therefore, since we are surrounded by such a great cloud of witnesses, let us throw off everything that hinders and the sin that so easily entangles. And let us run with perseverance the race marked out for us.

HEBREWS 12:1 (NIV)

Strive to do what is right in every circumstance. Be aware of your words and actions, and ask God to help you be an extension of His love and grace. Keep your eyes on Jesus and live your life by being the best person you can be.

Dear Lord, help me stay connected to You throughout this race here on earth.

Reflections

Unlikely Heroes

They were the heroes of old, men of renown.

GENESIS 6:4 (NIV)

The Bible is filled with unlikely heroes. Often God uses less-than-perfect people to inspire us. Ruth teaches loyalty. Noah teaches trust. Paul teaches perseverance. When you think that a goal is out of reach, look to the Bible and the many examples of people rising to the challenge and achieving good things even when they didn't feel worthy.

Heavenly Father, release the hero within me.

Reflections

Pray Out Your Doubt

Everything is possible for one who believes.

MARK 9:23 (NIV)

———————————

Anything is possible. The one requirement from you is that you must have faith. What a tremendous promise! If you can overcome doubt and really, deeply believe, you will begin to experience a transformed life where you witness miracles.

Lord, when I am in doubt, help me pray it out.

Reflections

Doodle Your Prayers

Ask and it will be given to you; seek and you will find; knock and the door will be opened to you. For everyone who asks receives; the one who seeks finds; and to the one who knocks, the door will be opened.

MATTHEW 7:7–8 (NIV)

Are you looking for a fun way to pray? Try drawing your prayers. Sketch a picture of what's on your mind or doodle your favorite scripture. As you etch His word in the space below, focus your heart on Him.

Heavenly Father, today I will put pen to paper and open my mind and heart to You.

Reflections

An Amazing
Work in Progress

Not that I have already obtained all this, or have already arrived at my goal, but I press on to take hold of that for which Christ Jesus took hold of me.

PHILIPPIANS 3:12 (NIV)

Life is a series of goals to reach and lessons to learn. Sometimes our trials may seem unclear and the lessons unresolved. In times of uncertainty, press forward and trust that your life is a beautiful, amazing work in progress.

Heavenly Father, help me learn to love the uncertainties and trials—the works in progress—that You are completing in my life.

Reflections

God Has Your Back

*No man shall be able to stand before you all the days
of your life. Just as I was with Moses, so I will be
with you. I will not leave you or forsake you.*

JOSHUA 1:5 (ESV)

When the going is hard and you feel discouraged or
frightened, turn to the verse above. Know that God
is with you. You are not alone. He will always protect,
guide, and comfort you. Whatever challenge lies ahead,
you can face it with confidence because he is with you.

*Heavenly Father, on days when I feel tested,
I know I can go on because You are with me.*

Reflections

Soak Up Jesus's Love

*But you, dear friends, carefully build yourselves
up in this most holy faith by praying in the Holy
Spirit, staying right at the center of God's love, keeping
your arms open and outstretched, ready for the
mercy of our Master, Jesus Christ. This is the
unending life, the real life!*

JUDE 1:20–21 (MSG)

———————◆———————

Do you approach Jesus with arms outstretched and
an open heart? This verse focuses on building your
faith by staying in the center of His glorious love. Take
a moment, close your eyes, and feel His abundant love.

*Heavenly Father, my arms are open and outstretched,
ready for Your mercy.*

Reflections

Your Life Is
Vastly Important

*In the same way, let your light shine before
others, so that they may see your good works and
give glory to your Father who is in heaven.*

MATTHEW 5:16 (ESV)

Today, make an effort to be a blessing to others—not
just close family members and friends, but people you
interact with throughout your day. Use every inter-
action as an opportunity to make the day brighter by
bringing His light to other's lives. Celebrate the positive
difference you make in the world.

*Dear Lord, I want to shine Your light. Guide me
where I am needed. Give me the grace to be kind
and patience to serve You well.*

Reflections

Judas's Betrayal

*"What will you give me if I deliver him over to you?"
And they paid him thirty pieces of silver. And from
that moment he sought an opportunity to betray him.*

MATTHEW 26:15–16 (ESV)

Judas, one of Jesus's chosen disciples, betrayed him. Today, consider what Christ went through. Look to your own life and look for all the ways—big and small—where you might be betraying Him. Is it turning away from something He's nudged you to do, or remaining quiet in situations where you feel His push to get involved? Are you being called to forgive someone who has betrayed you?

*Heavenly Father, be patient with me as I walk
with You. Know my heart is in the right place,
but sometimes it takes my actions time to catch up.*

Reflections

Sunbursts of Light

*The people who walked in darkness have seen
a great light. For those who lived in a land of
deep shadows—light! sunbursts of light!*

ISAIAH 9:2 (MSG)

On the next sunny day, take a moment to drink in its beauty—be mindful of the glorious light—and keep it in your heart for times when you feel as if you are walking in the dark. Know that it is because of faith that you can always walk in the light. Because of faith, your light can help others out of their own darkness.

*Heavenly Father, help me shine Your glorious
light on those around me.*

Reflections

Time to Laugh

A time to cry and a time to laugh.
A time to grieve and a time to dance.

ECCLESIASTES 3:4 (NLT)

Laughter is an amazing gift from God. When life gets you down, lighten up and look for the humor in stressful situations. A good laugh can make a dreary day brighter. Live with laughter in your heart and let the silly side of a situation lift your spirit.

Heavenly Father, when I'm stressed and looking at life too seriously, guide me to see the silly side. Guide me to laughter.

Reflections

The Source of Courage

Do you not know? Have you not heard? The LORD is the everlasting God, the Creator of the ends of the earth. He will not grow tired or weary, and his understanding no one can fathom. He gives strength to the weary and increases the power of the weak.

ISAIAH 40:28–29 (NIV)

There will be times when you need courage to keep you going when the going is hard. Tap into the Source of courage by feeling God's presence. Hear Him say, "I am with you always."

Lord Jesus, I know that You will give me strength and courage to face my fears.

Reflections

Pray Every Day

Give us today our daily bread.

MATTHEW 6:11 (NIV)

Jesus knew we needed to pray each day. He gave us the words, "Give us today our daily bread" as a model for living. Share all of your cares with Him. Ask Him to give you what you need to sustain you from day to day. Make your needs known to Him and trust He will provide.

Heavenly Father, thank You for being here
for me today as I pour out my soul to You.
Here is what is on my mind…

Reflections

Lose Spiritual Weight

*Let us also lay aside every weight, and sin
which clings so closely, and let us run with
endurance the race that is set before us.*

HEBREWS 12:1 (ESV)

One way to get more energy is to lay aside the heavy weights that sap your strength—burdens such as fear, hate, anger, impatience, and all types of sin. In fact, sin is the heaviest of all weights, and it must be laid aside to continue forward on your spiritual journey.

*Dear Jesus, help me let go of the things that bring me
down. Energize my spirit with Your light.*

Reflections

Crush Your Goals

*Now finish the work, so that your eager
willingness to do it may be matched by
your completion of it, according to your means.*

2 CORINTHIANS 8:11 (NIV)

Do you need a little bit of inspiration to help you reach your goals? Take heart! Although Jesus calls us to endure, He also promises to work in and through us. "Being confident of this, that he who began a good work in you will carry it on to completion until the day of Christ Jesus" (Philippians 1:6, NIV).

*Heavenly Father, inspire me to carry on prayerfully
as I work toward reaching my goals.*

Reflections

The Name Above Every Name

Therefore God has highly exalted him and bestowed on him the name that is above every name.

PHILIPPIANS 2:9 (ESV)

The Bible is filled with names for Jesus. Isaiah calls Jesus "Wonderful Counselor, Mighty God, Everlasting Father, Prince of Peace" (9:6). Each specific name comforts and sustains us during different seasons of our lives. The Bread of Life (John 6:35) will nourish your hungry spirit. The Good Shepherd (John 10:11) will guide you on your way. And when all seems dark, the Light of the World is there for you (John 8:12).

Thank You, Jesus. You hold the name that is above every name.

Reflections

The Unshakeable Truth

Yet in all these things we are more than conquerors through Him who loved us.

ROMANS 8:37 (NKJV)

Build up your spirit, day by day, with the power of God's presence in your life and His eternal love for you. No matter what happens, nothing can separate you from His love and protection. He understands you completely and will never forsake you.

Lord God, I will dwell on this verse until it becomes an unshakeable truth in my life.

Reflections

The Breath of Life

This is what the Sovereign Lord *says to these bones:
I will make breath enter you, and you will come to life.*

EZEKIEL 37:5 (NIV)

Your great hopes, dreams, and ideals are not dead if you let God breathe the breath of fresh spiritual life into them. The spirit of God can revitalize anything. With God, life can always be vital, always dynamic. Life is renewable.

*Dear Lord, thank You for my life, my breath,
and all the blessings of this very moment.*

Reflections

Be Strong

David also said to Solomon his son, "Be strong and courageous, and do the work. Do not be afraid or discouraged, for the Lord God, my God, is with you."

1 CHRONICLES 28:20 (NIV)

God told His people dozens of times, "Be strong." Perhaps He tells us this because He knows He asks grand things from us, but also because He knows it can be human nature to get discouraged. Are there big plans in your life that you abandoned because they seemed too challenging? Revisit them now with God's Word to propel you forward.

Dear Lord, help me find the courage and strength to carry out Your plans.

Reflections

Well-Done Prayer

His master replied, "Well done, good and faithful servant! You have been faithful with a few things; I will put you in charge of many things. Come and share your master's happiness!"

MATTHEW 25:21 (NIV)

Do you have the heart of a servant in all that you do? Are you using the abilities, gifts, and resources that you have been given to bring glory to the Lord? Ask God to show you ways you can be of service. Whenever you feel a task is too big, ask Him for help.

Heavenly Father, help me live so that I am one day welcomed to heaven with the words, "Well done!"

Reflections

God's Love

As the Father has loved me, so have I loved you.
Now remain in my love.

JOHN 15:9 (NIV)

W hen you need encouragement that God really loves you, turn to the book of John. John was called the one whom Jesus loved. This Gospel's message is that love is the redeeming power that is available to all who turn to God. As people of faith, we can spread His message and His love.

Lord, show me how I can spread Your love here on earth.

Reflections

See Everyday Miracles

For this people's heart has grown dull, and with their ears they can barely hear, and their eyes they have closed, lest they should see with their eyes and hear with their ears and understand with their heart and turn, and I would heal them.

MATTHEW 13:15–16 (ESV)

Just because your eyes are open doesn't mean you can see. You must open your awareness to see God in the everyday blessings that are often overlooked. All good things are made from the Lord. Today, slow down and take notice of the many ways He shines His light on your life.

Heavenly Father, today I will keep my eyes open and see the many ways You bless me.

Reflections

Write Your Legacy

No one was sorry when he died.

2 CHRONICLES 21:20 (NLT)

The above verse was said about King Jehoram, a ruler who lived a life of greed and power, a life totally apart from God. In contrast, consider the Apostle Paul's "epitaph," which he himself wrote in a final letter: "I have fought the good fight, I have finished the race, and I have remained faithful. And now the prize awaits me—the crown of righteousness, which the Lord, the righteous Judge, will give me on the day of his return" (2 Timothy 4:7-8, NLT). How do you want to be remembered? It's never too late or too early to live your best life.

Lord, I want my life to be one of purpose—a generous life filled with meaning; a faith-filled life of service.

Reflections

Judge Less, Love More

*Let love and faithfulness never leave
you; bind them around your neck, write
them on the tablet of your heart.*

PROVERBS 3:3 (NIV)

Everyone knows you can't judge a book by its cover, and yet sometimes we make rushed judgments that aren't backed up by the right information. The next time you are about to place a negative label on someone, stop for a moment and look for the Christ in them. See the good and extend a kind word.

*Lord, help me choose loving thoughts. Guide me
to compassion and away from criticism, so that
I may walk humbly beside You.*

Reflections

The Time Is Now

This is the day the LORD has made.
We will rejoice and be glad in it.

PSALM 118:24 (NLT)

———————————

Do you find yourself caught up in "if only" thoughts when you consider your own happiness? "I'd be happy if only I had more money...a better house...a few less pounds here or there." Although it's healthy and good to have goals and to strive to improve your life, your happiness shouldn't be delayed by circumstances. Every day is an opportunity to appreciate where you are and what you are at this exact moment.

Dear God, today may Your glory be manifested in my
life—a day full of grace, joy, happiness, and laughter.

Reflections

Right a Wrong

*Bear with each other and forgive one another
if any of you has a grievance against someone.
Forgive as the Lord forgave you.*

COLOSSIANS 3:13 (NIV)

When you have been wronged, do you let resentment tie up your life in knots? Don't let animosity sap you of strength and sidetrack you from moving forward. Pray to be free of hard-hearted feelings. When you have hurt another with some action or omission, ask for forgiveness. Then, whether you receive it or not, put the experience behind you.

*Lord, help me overlook others' faults in the hope
that they will overlook mine.*

Reflections

Build Sandcastles

On a good day, enjoy yourself; on a bad day, examine your conscience. God arranges for both kinds of days so that we won't take anything for granted.

ECCLESIASTES 7:14 (MSG)

Building sandcastles is sometimes used as a metaphor for wasting your time. Yet sandcastles serve an important purpose: they allow us to create something that we know will not last; they encourage us to savor the present moment. Some days that's exactly what we need.

Heavenly Father, remind me that it is never a waste to be playful and to enjoy the day.

Reflections

Perspective Takes Time

God is just: He will pay back trouble to those who trouble you and give relief to you who are troubled.

2 THESSALONIANS 1:6–7 (NIV)

Life can be frustrating. Sometimes bad things happen that we don't understand. We lose a job, a loved one becomes ill, we suffer a blow that leaves us asking, "Why did this happen?" Instead of straining to see meaning or trying to figure out what's happening when you're in the eye of the storm, recognize that wisdom and growth takes time. Perspective is everything. Have faith and trust God's plan.

Heavenly Father, I know I must let go of needing to understand everything. Help me stop asking why, place my trust in You, and accept what is.

Reflections

Be Confident!

*Be strong and courageous. Do not be afraid;
do not be discouraged, for the Lord your
God will be with you wherever you go.*

JOSHUA 1:9 (NIV)

When you need a boost of bravery, build your confidence by repeating the above verse. Pray that the Lord will empower you with great strength. Visualize His strength flowing into you. Look upon life's challenges with excitement and enthusiasm knowing that God is with you.

*Dear Lord, let me feel close to You. In this moment,
help me feel Your strength.*

Reflections

Good Night Verse

Do not be anxious about anything, but in every situation, by prayer and petition, with thanksgiving, present your requests to God. And the peace of God, which transcends all understanding, will guard your hearts and your minds in Christ Jesus.

PHILIPPIANS 4:6–7 (NIV)

On nights when you can't sleep, when the worries of tomorrow or rehashing a hard day keep you awake, turn to this scripture. Offer your worries to the One who can do something about them. Tell Him what is on your mind and ask Him to guard your heart and help you find rest. Feel His perfect peace cover you.

Heavenly Father, thank You for protecting my thoughts and helping me trust You with my worries.

Reflections

Raise Your Spirits

*Where can I go from your Spirit? Where can I flee
from your presence? If I go up to the heavens, you are
there; if I make my bed in the depths, you are there.*

PSALM 139:7–8 (NIV)

———————

When the world seems to focus on hatred, resentment, and failure, lift your eyes to high places and know that "my help comes from the Lord" (Psalm 121:2, NIV). Remind yourself that doom and gloom are temporary, and fill your mind with God. Let His positive energy flow into you. Remind yourself that life is fascinating, beautiful, and good every day, all your days.

*Our Heavenly Father, fill me with the radiant
positive power of Jesus Christ.*

Reflections

Change Takes Time

*Put on the new self, created to be like
God in true righteousness and holiness.*

EPHESIANS 4:24 (NIV)

———————◆———————

Sometimes spiritual growth happens overnight. Most times, it is a gradual process that takes patience and dedication. Don't be discouraged if your faith walk hasn't progressed as far as you hoped. God isn't in a hurry!

*Heavenly Father, if I feel discouraged or troubled
by doubt and disbelief, help me to remember
that faith is patient.*

Reflections

The God of Hope

*May the God of hope fill you with all joy and peace
as you trust in him, so that you may overflow
with hope by the power of the Holy Spirit.*

ROMANS 15:13 (NIV)

Catherine Marshall said, "God is the only one who can make the valley of trouble a door of hope." It's difficult to be filled with hope when you are plagued by adversity. When your heart is troubled, read the above scripture and remind yourself that God can turn problems into possibilities. Let your heart overflow with hope.

*Dear Lord, help me to let go of passing challenges
so that I can fill my heart with Your limitless hope.*

Reflections

God's Grace

Looking diligently lest any man fail of the grace of God; lest any root of bitterness springing up trouble you, and thereby many be defiled.

HEBREWS 12:15 (KJV)

In Isaiah 38:15 (CEB), King Hezekiah wrote: "I will wander my whole life with a bitter spirit." Yet when Hezekiah called out to God, his bitterness was exchanged for wholeness. When your mood needs improving, look to the Lord and become whole.

Lord, when I become consumed with bitterness, I will call out to You and trade it in for the wholeness of Your grace.

Reflections

Look to the Clouds

*After he said this, he was taken up before their
very eyes, and a cloud hid him from their sight.*

ACTS 1:9 (NIV)

In this scripture, and in different passages throughout the Bible, clouds symbolize divine presence. Other
examples are when Moses ascended Mount Sinai and
a cloud covered the mountain, or at Solomon's dedication when a cloud filled the temple. The next cloudy day,
pause to reflect on God's use of clouds to remind us of
His presence and to feel His comfort when it is overcast.

*Heavenly Father, help me feel Your presence,
in both cloudy and cloudless skies.*

Reflections

Borrowed Things

He must increase, but I must decrease.

JOHN 3:30 (ESV)

Norman Vincent Peale said, "Did it ever occur to you that you do not really own a thing, not a single thing? You are entrusted by the Lord according to your own ability to handle some of His goods for a while. If you use things selfishly for yourself, you will probably lose them and you will certainly lose the values that would come to you if you would use them for God."

Heavenly Father, free me of selfish thoughts and deeds.

Reflections

Shape the Future

For as he thinks in his heart, so is he.

PROVERBS 23:7 (NKJV)

Your thoughts have tremendous power. They can work for you or against you; they can help you achieve great victories or lead you down the road to inglorious defeat. Be aware of how your thinking is shaping your future. Look to God to help you believe in your abilities so that you can become your best.

Lord, give me the vision to see myself as You would have me be. Give me the wisdom to let You run my life.

Reflections

Conquer Your Giants

*Now therefore, give me this mountain of which the
Lord spoke in that day; for you heard in that day how
the Anakim were there, and that the cities were great
and fortified. It may be that the Lord will be with me,
and I shall be able to drive them out as the Lord said.*

JOSHUA 14:12 (NKJV)

Do you ever feel as if you are standing at the foot of a
mountain, wondering if you can conquer your giants?
Fear can convince you to back down and surrender
before you even try. With Jesus's help, you can stand
your ground and tackle anything!

*Lord Jesus, no matter what I think are my limitations,
with Your help I can be victorious!*

Reflections

Joy in Uncertain Times

*You have put more joy in my heart than they have
when their grain and wine abound.*

PSALM 4:7 (ESV)

Uncertainty, like change, is a word that makes most
people uncomfortable. We want to know what is coming, and we often make the mistake of thinking we
can't relax or be joyful if we don't know what tomorrow
brings. Trusting God is the cure to fearing the unknown.
When your faith is strong, you can celebrate right now,
trusting the future is in His hands.

*Heavenly Father, my joy doesn't depend on
my circumstances; it depends on You.*

Reflections

The Joy of Jesus in Your Life

But let all who take refuge in you be glad; let them ever sing for joy. Spread your protection over them, that those who love your name may rejoice in you.

PSALM 5:11 (NIV)

Happiness is usually tied to life's circumstances, but joy is quite different. Joy isn't simply an emotion. Joy is having a relationship with Jesus and knowing that because of His presence in your life, everything will be okay. Regardless of chaos and difficulties, your abiding faith will see you through.

Dear Lord, I have faith that You are working everything out for me.

Reflections

A Time for Prayer

Pray all the time.

1 THESSALONIANS 5:17 (MSG)

Think of every moment as an opportunity to pray. Pray the first thing in the morning. Pray while you're in the car or walking about. Don't worry about what to say or if you should be sharing things that may seem small or trivial. Invite Jesus to help guide the details of your life. Pray, pray, and keep on praying.

*Heavenly Father, I want to make
every moment a prayer to You.*

Reflections

Fill Your Spirit

Jesus answered her, "If you knew the gift of God and who it is that asks you for a drink, you would have asked him and he would have given you living water."

JOHN 4:10 (NIV)

God is always available to us when our souls are parched. We only need to ask Him for His healing streams. If you feel weary, read the Bible and draw close to Christ. He can quench your heart's thirst and help you feel spiritually fulfilled.

Thank You, God, for satisfying my thirsty soul with Your life-giving Spirit. Remind me to come to You when I feel like I'm running on empty.

Reflections

Give Your Worries to God

*Cast your cares on the Lord and he will sustain you;
he will never let the righteous be shaken.*

PSALM 55:22 (NIV)

Is something bothering you? Loosen your fingers on the problem and release the situation into God's hands. God is your refuge and strength. He is your very present help. Open up and let Him in.

*Dear Lord, this message is so simple, and yet
so often I just don't let go. Help me change this
about myself, starting right now.*

Reflections

Step into the Light

When Jesus spoke again to the people, he said, "I am the light of the world. Whoever follows me will never walk in darkness, but will have the light of life."

JOHN 8:12 (NIV)

When you are downcast and discouraged, know that God sent His only Son to illuminate your path. Jesus is always with you. He is present in every moment of every day. He can guide you to live the life He wants you to live—a life of light and love! Visualize a bright beam of God's love protecting, guiding, and healing you.

Lord Jesus, shine Your radiance on all aspects of my life.

Reflections

Love with All You've Got

Jesus replied: "'Love the Lord your God with all your heart and with all your soul and with all your mind.' This is the first and greatest commandment. And the second is like it: 'Love your neighbor as yourself.'"

MATTHEW 22:37–39 (NIV)

Jesus asks us to love with our whole being, our whole heart, and all our soul and mind. When we love as Jesus models, we can heal the deepest hurts, overcome the toughest challenges, and accomplish the greatest things. Pray this verse when you need more love in your life.

Dear God, please let my life be filled with love.

Reflections

Pray God's Word

The Lord is my shepherd; I shall not want.

PSALM 23:1 (KJV)

The twenty-third psalm is composed of 118 words and is easy to memorize. Perhaps you already know it by heart. But the psalm's power is not in memorizing the words, but rather in taking in its positive and hopeful approach to life verse by verse. Pray God's words back to Him, and experience His goodness. Be strengthened by His promises.

Lord, You are my Shepherd; I shall not want. Thou makest me to lie down in green pastures: Thou leadest me beside the still waters. Thou restorest my soul...

Reflections

Your Best Self

*These [trials] have come so that the proven genuine-
ness of your faith—of greater worth than gold, which
perishes even though refined by fire—may result in
praise, glory and honor when Jesus Christ is revealed.*

1 PETER 1:7 (NIV)

Although you cannot control everything that happens
in your life, you can control how you react to challenges.
When you approach life's storms as learning experiences
that will help make you a stronger and better person,
you can see the silver lining of every cloud.

*Dear Lord, guide me to be an eager student of life—to
see every struggle as a tool to shape me into my best.*

Reflections

The Wisdom of Not Knowing

*Let the wise hear and increase in learning, and
the one who understands obtain guidance.*

PROVERBS 1:5 (ESV)

It is okay to not know everything. To not know what
you want or how to make things better. When you say, "I
don't know," it opens the door to finding out, to thinking and discovering, to praying for an answer. So the
next time you feel foolish or confused because you don't
know, step back and wait, be patient. Ask for God's help.

*Heavenly Father, I don't have all the answers, but I
know that You do. Teach me to live in Your wisdom.*

Reflections

Every Good and Perfect Gift

*Every good and perfect gift is from above, coming
down from the Father of the heavenly lights,
who does not change like shifting shadows.*

JAMES 1:17 (NIV)

Everything you have is a gift from God—your family, home, career—everything! Don't take anything for granted. Reflect on the many blessings He has bestowed on you. Praise Him for the comfort and indescribable hope He gives you.

*Father of Light, thank You for the heavenly
gifts You bring to my life.*

Reflections

Live to the Fullest

The steadfast love of the LORD never ceases; his mercies never come to an end; they are new every morning; great is your faithfulness.

LAMENTATIONS 3:22–23 (ESV)

God's interest in you is fresh every morning. Rely on His loving care, and life with all its challenges will become easier. Starting right now, live each moment to the fullest!

Dear Lord, guide me to make the most of every hour. Help me view each sunrise as a new opportunity to shine and each sunset as a time to reflect.

Reflections

Come, Lord Jesus

Come, Lord Jesus.

REVELATION 22:20 (NIV)

Today's verse is the last prayer recorded in the Bible. When you need help, turn to these words, not only as a prayer for Christ's return, but also as a prayer for His presence and grace to guide you through whatever problem or situation you face.

Today and every day may I pray, "Come, Lord Jesus."

Reflections

The Grace of Forgiveness

If you, GOD, kept records on wrongdoings, who would stand a chance? As it turns out, forgiveness is your habit, and that's why you're worshiped.

PSALM 130:3–4 (MSG)

Mistakes, hurt feelings, and wrongdoings are part of being human, but the good news is that confession brings God's grace. Because of Jesus's promise to forgive, no matter how many mistakes we make or problems we create, we can still receive His ever-renewing mercies.

Lord God, thank You for forgiving me—for lifting guilt from my heart and filling me with Your grace.

Reflections

All You Really Need

Jesus answered, "I am the way and the truth and the life. No one comes to the Father except through me."

JOHN 14:6 (NIV)

We often make life a lot more complicated than it truly is. Simply put, Jesus is all we need. Corrie ten Boom said, "You don't really know Jesus is all you need until Jesus is all you have." You don't need to wait for life's difficulties to bring you to a place where you are ready to truly accept and understand the power of Jesus. Open the door to your heart and spirit, for He is "the way and the truth and the life."

Lord Jesus, when I am distracted by life's busyness, guide my focus back to You.

Reflections

Practice Self-Control

*Then Jesus told his disciples, "If anyone
would come after me, let him deny himself
and take up his cross and follow me."*

MATTHEW 16:24 (ESV)

Norman Vincent Peale said, "The more small pleasures a person gives up to concentrate on one important task, the stronger he becomes. Jesus Christ was the
greatest example of One Who depended on self-denial
for strength to perform his ministry."

*Lord, help me remember that the ultimate in
self-control is not for me to become master of
my fate, but to be able to serve You.*

Reflections

A Gentle Answer

A gentle answer turns away wrath,
but a harsh word stirs up anger.

PROVERBS 15:1 (NIV)

———————◆———————

Next time you are tempted to speak harshly against another who has hurt you, stop for a moment. Is the problem as serious as you're making it? Will your words improve the situation and lead to a solution, or will they only show your anger? Whatever you say, be compassionate and caring. Set your mind on mending the relationship.

Keep me, God, from stirring up anger.
Help me use words that comfort and heal.

Reflections

God Is Well

Therefore put on the full armor of God, so that when the day of evil comes, you may be able to stand your ground, and after you have done everything, to stand.

EPHESIANS 6:13 (NIV)

Sometimes fear and panic can paralyze your spirit and make you feel helpless. If this happens, say, "Heavenly Father, help me trust myself completely to Your healing hands and to rest in Your great love." Align your will and your spirit with His full armor and divine power.

Heavenly Father, when negative thinking and worries plague me, help me remember that I stand with You.

Reflections

A Quick Pick-Me-Up

*Hallelujah! Praise God from heaven, praise him
from the mountaintops; Praise Him, all you his
angels, praise him, all you his warriors . . . Praise,
oh let them praise the name of GOD—he spoke
the word, and there they were!*

PSALM 148:1–5 (MSG)

Does your spirit need a boost? Don't reach for a coffee
or an energy drink. Instead, spend a few minutes praising Jesus. Invite His joy to fill you. Praise Jesus for Who
He is, what He's done, and what He has promised to do.

*Heavenly Father, thank You for being my victorious
Savior, best Friend, and holy Lord.*

Reflections

Jesus's Prayer

"I pray for them. I am not praying for the world, but for those you have given me, for they are yours. . . . My prayer is not for them alone. I pray also for those who will believe in me through their message. . . . Father, I want those you have given me to be with me where I am. . . ."

JOHN 17:9, 20, 24 (NIV)

When you read John chapter 17, you discover that Jesus prayed for protection, joy, and unity for His followers. If you are feeling overwhelmed, say the above verse and take comfort in Jesus's prayer. Know that He is on your side.

Dear Jesus, Your prayers are a great blessing to me.

Reflections

Your #1 Priority

*But seek first the kingdom of God and His righteousness,
and all these things shall be added to you.*

MATTHEW 6:33 (NKJV)

Every once in a while, it's good to take time to reflect on our goals. If you are feeling off track, or if you simply need direction in your life, turn to this verse. Make God your first priority. Spend time with Him. Share your hopes and dreams and ask Him to help you stay motivated and focused.

*Heavenly Father, give me the insight to seek purpose
and meaning in my life through You.*

Reflections

When God Says No

The LORD will fulfill his purpose for me;
your steadfast love, O LORD, endures forever.

PSALM 138:8 (NRSV)

There are times in life when despite trying your hardest, praying earnestly, and deeply desiring something, it
just doesn't happen. Sometimes you must accept that
not everything is available when you want it. When this
happens, you must trust that something better—something different than you expected—is on its way.

Father God, it's hard to let go of certain wants, but
I will because I trust Your plan and Your timing.

Reflections

Mother's Love

And Mary said: "My soul glorifies the Lord and my spirit rejoices in God my Savior, for he has been mindful of the humble state of his servant. From now on, all generations will call me blessed, for the Mighty One has done great things for me—holy is his name."

LUKE 1:46–49 (NIV)

When we think about our mothers, we can look to the above verse. Mary, the mother of Jesus, is the most beloved and revered woman in the Bible. She willingly accepted her role as the blessed mother and remained stalwart in her faith.

Dear Lord, You have done so many great things for me . . . most especially, You have blessed me with a mother's love.

Reflections

Safe Travels

The LORD *will watch over your coming and going both now and forevermore.*

PSALM 121:8 (NIV)

———————————◆———————————

There are so many reasons to travel: to be with friends and family, for work, to help others, or just for fun. Whether you're going on a business trip or just running an errand, don't let stress steal your joy. Relax with this verse and know that God will guide your journey.

Dear Lord, keep me safely sheltered in Your protecting arms.

Reflections

When the Bible Is
Hard to Understand

*Then Jesus took them through the writings of Moses
and all the prophets, explaining from all the Scriptures
the things concerning himself.*

LUKE 24:27 (NLT)

Are there parts of the Bible you've been avoiding because they seem too difficult to understand? Instead of skipping scripture that has you puzzled, turn to a confusing passage and ask God to reveal His truth to you. Pray for Him to show Himself in the words.

*Heavenly Father, I know You want to explain
Yourself to me. Speak to my heart. Reveal Your truth.*

Reflections

Look Up and Out

*I lift up my eyes to the mountains—where does my
help come from? My help comes from the Lord,
the Maker of heaven and earth.*

PSALM 121:1–2 (NIV)

When you are feeling down or alone, change your focus
from yourself to something or someone else. By looking
outward, you'll find strengthening reminders that God
cares for you. Raise your eyes upward—you'll seldom see
a rainbow or a bluebird by looking at your feet.

*Lord, the Maker of heaven and earth, help me refocus
and lift my eyes to see the big picture of life.*

Reflections

Celebrate Life

*You make known to me the path of life; in
your presence there is fullness of joy; at your
right hand are pleasures forevermore.*

PSALM 16:11 (ESV)

Take time to celebrate your accomplishments and your
spiritual growth! You are a child of God. Your beauty is
within you. Celebrate the lessons you've learned and the
blessings that await you. Celebrate life!

*Heavenly Father, I praise You for this great gift of life!
Thank You for everything. Thank You for my past,
which has shaped me into who I am, and thank You
for my future filled with new opportunities. I praise
You for all the blessings I receive on the way.*

Reflections

Seeing the Light

And as he journeyed, he came near Damascus:
and suddenly there shined round about
him a light from heaven.

ACTS 9:3 (KJV)

In this verse Saul had an amazing and incredible experience, one that changed him from being a persecutor of early Christians to a follower of Christ. Perhaps you have had a less dramatic, yet no less important, experience. Reflect on your life, and think about a time that God singled you out to reveal His light of truth.

Thank You, Lord, for sending Your truth to me.

Reflections

Nothing Is Beyond God's Forgiveness

But I say to you, love your enemies, bless those who curse you, do good to those who hate you, and pray for those who spitefully use you and persecute you.

MATTHEW 5:44 (NKJV)

One thing is certain: when Judas realized the evil of his actions, he was so full of guilt that he could not live with himself. What he forgot was that Jesus would have forgiven him even for his betrayal. If you feel as if you've failed God, remember that there is no sin beyond His forgiveness.

Dear Lord, thank You for the grace of Your love, which heals our guilt and takes away our sins.

Reflections

The Key to Fulfillment

Whoever finds their life will lose it, and whoever loses their life for my sake will find it.

MATTHEW 10:39 (NIV)

God wants you to have a blessed and wonderful life. To accomplish this, He calls each of us to do His work here on earth. The key to fulfillment is to give yourself totally to a cause and be focused on and dedicated to worthwhile tasks.

Father, fulfill Your purposes for me and help me to give myself generously to others without reservation.

Reflections

Silent Change

My God, my God, why have You forsaken me? Why are You so far from saving me, from the words of my groaning? O my God, I cry by day, but you do not answer, and by night, but I find no rest.

PSALM 22:1–2 (ESV)

In times when God seems silent, when you feel as if your prayers are going unanswered, change is happening behind the scenes. Even if you can't feel it, you are growing. You're developing a deeper faith and a greater knowing. Believe and trust the calm, strong insight that often comes in times we feel God is silent.

Dear Lord, in quiet times, when I doubt that You are near, hold me close and comfort me; reassure me there is nothing to fear.

Reflections

Prayer of Relinquishment

*On the day I called, you answered me;
my strength of soul you increased.*

PSALM 138:3 (ESV)

Catherine Marshall said, "When you relinquish everything to God, you stop commanding and demanding God to do things for you. As long as you keep telling God what to do, He will honor your free will and will not violate it even to answer your prayer."

*Lord, I truly and completely surrender my problem
to You. I need faith right now to see blessings instead of
fears. Thank You for Your promises and provision!*

Reflections

What's Your Spiritual Age?

*But grow in the grace and knowledge of our Lord
and Savior Jesus Christ. To him be the glory both
now and to the day of eternity. Amen.*

2 PETER 3:18 (ESV)

Your spiritual growth continues until you enter into eternity. Regardless of your chronological age, your spiritual age depends on your dedication to your faith. And unlike the negative connotation of old age, having an old spiritual age is a precious gift!

Loving Father, I long to be led by Your heart. It is my deepest desire to grow spiritually each and every day.

Reflections

Scripture to Fight Fear

The LORD is my light and my salvation—whom shall I fear? The Lord is the stronghold of my life—of whom shall I be afraid?

PSALM 27:1 (NIV)

Fear thrives on darkness—dark thoughts, dark attitudes. The good news is that God's Word can flood the darkness with light. Fill your mind with His strength, power, and positive thoughts and drive out any fears that haunt you.

Dear Lord, thank You for shining Your bright and brilliant light on me and replacing my worries with faith.

Reflections

Picture a Positive Outcome

Where there is no vision, the people perish:
but he that keepeth the law, happy is he.

PROVERBS 29:18 (KJV)

A successful approach to accomplishing a goal is to picture yourself having already achieved it. Visualize a positive outcome. If you can see something in your mind, it's easier to believe it is possible, and anything is possible if you can believe.

Lord, guide me to pursue worthy goals,
and help me reach them.

Reflections

Share Your Problems

*Therefore confess your sins to each other and pray
for each other so that you may be healed.*

JAMES 5:16 (NIV)

There is a reason that God asks us to confess our sins
to one another. It's not to shame us, but rather to share
our burdens. When we honestly discuss our trials and
troubles with others, we help one another heal.

*Lord, thank You for helping me see that sharing
my problems helps me to trust and heal.*

Reflections

The Power of the Shortest Verse

Jesus wept.

JOHN 11:35 (NIV)

John 11:35 is the shortest verse in the Bible, but its depth of meaning is vast. In times of sorrow, find comfort in this verse and knowing that Jesus is with you. He is filled with compassion and understanding of what you are going through. When you weep, He weeps with you. You are not alone.

Father, no tear escapes Your notice.
When sorrows come, comfort me with Your love.

Reflections

Pray, Hope, Wait

*Be joyful in hope, patient in affliction,
faithful in prayer.*

ROMANS 12:12 (NIV)

Franciscan friar Padre Pio said, "Pray, hope, and don't worry." Prayer is the key to every problem. If you are discouraged or worried about something, open your heart and let your prayers flow heavenward. With the Lord's help, you can endure every challenge. Be patient and wait.

*Heavenly Father, I thank You for the gift of prayer,
which calms my troubled mind by shining
Your glorious light on my dark thoughts.*

Reflections

Grow Your Faith

*And the seed that fell on good soil represents those
who hear and accept God's word and produce
a harvest of thirty, sixty, or even a hundred
times as much as had been planted!*

MARK 4:20 (NLT)

As every gardener knows, the best seed cannot do well unless the soil is prepared. God wants us to be "good soil" so that our hearts can receive His Word. Allow Him to pull the weeds that block you from His love and to help you see the purpose of the struggles in your life.

*Heavenly Father, till my spirit and guide
me to nurture Your Word in my life.*

Reflections

Battles Become Blessings

*He will cover you with his feathers, and under his
wings you will find refuge; his faithfulness will be
your shield and rampart. You will not fear the terror
of night, nor the arrow that flies by day.*

PSALM 91:4–5 (NIV)

The Lord makes a way for you, even when you don't see
a way. Cling to Him tightly, knowing that He will protect and defend you. When you seek Him and trust His
perfect will, life's battles become blessings.

*Heavenly Father, You are my shield—cover me
with Your grace and peace.*

Reflections

Jesus Knows

*Because he himself suffered when he was tempted,
he is able to help those who are being tempted.*

HEBREWS 2:18 (NIV)

W hatever trial, loss, or temptation you are going through, Jesus knows. There is nothing too hard, painful, or devastating for Him to identify with. When you bring your suffering to Him in prayer, He feels your pain as you feel His comfort.

*Heavenly Father, on days when I feel tested,
I know I can go on because You are with me.*

Reflections

The Power of Belief

That is why we labor and strive, because we have
put our hope in the living God, who is the Savior of
all people, and especially of those who believe.

1 TIMOTHY 4:10 (NIV)

Believe. That one word taken to heart can change your
life. Believe in God's power to transform you and situations around you. Believe in yourself and the talents God
gave you. Believe, and there is no limit to what you can
accomplish. Make an effort to say, "I believe I can" whenever a challenge arises, and expect spectacular results.

Lord, I believe!

Reflections

The Keynote of Your Day

I have rejoiced in your laws as much as in riches.

PSALM 119:14 (NLT)

Make Scripture the keynote of your day. Calm your mind and let His word take root in your heart. Be consistent and patient. Daily Bible reading will draw you into deep reflection as you apply His message to your life.

*Lord, thank You for the joy, beauty,
and wisdom of Your Word. Amen.*

Reflections

Pray Like Jabez

Jabez cried out to the God of Israel, "Oh, that you would bless me and enlarge my territory! Let your hand be with me, and keep me from harm so that I will be free from pain." And God granted his request.

1 CHRONICLES 4:10 (NIV)

God has a future filled with blessings planned for you. Seek His gifts not for your personal fulfillment but for His glory. When you rely on His multitude of gifts, you open a channel for His divine work to flow in and through your life.

Dear God, Thank You for blessing my life, for comforting my heart with Your love, and for strengthening my faith with Your Word. Thank You for everything.

Reflections

Are You Chasing the Wind?

I have seen all the things that are done under the sun;
all of them are meaningless, a chasing after the wind.

ECCLESIASTES 1:14 (NIV)

The book of Job reminds us that knowledge isn't everything. Yes, knowledge is a helpful and necessary tool, yet it doesn't serve every purpose. Likewise, the above scripture tells us that a life of meaning, purpose, and fulfillment is only found when we look to God.

Heavenly Father, You are the one who holds my future
in Your hands. Everything else is just chasing the wind.

Reflections

Healing Prayer

*The prayer of faith will restore the one who is
sick, and the Lord will raise him up, and if he has
committed sins, they will be forgiven him.*

JAMES 5:15 (NASB)

When you are facing emotional or physical pain, pray.
Ask Him to turn your discomforts into comforts and
sorrows to pleasures. Thank God for His love and the
many ways He enriches your life.

*Heavenly Father, let me feel Your healing
power move through me.*

Reflections

A Work of His Hands

*I am the vine, you are the branches. He who
abides in Me, and I in him, bears much fruit;
for without Me you can do nothing.*

JOHN 15:5 (NKJV)

Norman Vincent Peale said, "Have great hopes and dare to go all out for them. Have great dreams and dare to live them. Have tremendous expectations and believe in them." Too often we underestimate our own potential and set our sights too low. God has planted seeds that require work and faith to blossom. With faith and work, nothing is impossible.

*Inspire me, Lord, to dream big and
to support my dreams with action.*

Reflections

Call Forth the Riches
of Everyday Life

*You turned my wailing into dancing; you removed
my sackcloth and clothed me with joy.*

PSALM 30:11 (NIV)

Poet Rainer Maria Rilke said, "If your daily life seems poor, do not blame it; blame yourself, tell yourself that you are not poet enough to call forth its riches; for to the creator there is no poverty and no poor indifferent place." Make today the day when you call forth the riches of everyday life.

*Heavenly Father, I fall into the rut of believing I am
stuck or not living my best life. Help me to recognize that
with Your help, I can make the best of every situation.*

Reflections

Keep Me in Your Prayers

*Carry each other's burdens, and in this way
you will fulfill the law of Christ.*

GALATIANS 6:2 (NIV)

When you are feeling alone and vulnerable, reach out to others and ask them for prayer. God wants us to help one another, to carry each other's burdens. Prayer is one of God's greatest gifts.

*Heavenly Father, thank You for the comfort I feel
knowing I am held securely in a community of prayer.*

Reflections

See God's Love

The LORD appeared to us in the past, saying: "I have loved you with an everlasting love; I have drawn you with unfailing kindness."

JEREMIAH 31:3 (NIV)

God constantly sends messages of His love. Little reminders are sprinkled throughout the day—in the sky; the chirping of the birds; a single, heart-shaped leaf; the perfect song on the radio. His beauty and love are all around us. Today, make it a point to take notice. His messages of love are always there.

Heavenly Father, today I will seek, see, and be grateful for the many ways You show Your love.

Reflections

The Lord Is Your Rock

*From the ends of the earth, I cry to you for
help when my heart is overwhelmed. Lead me
to the towering rock of safety.*

PSALM 61:2 (NLT)

God is your strength. When you are sheltered in the truth of His Word and in the sanctuary of His presence, the stress that once overwhelmed you suddenly shrinks down to the pebble size it really is. Entrust Him with your problems and ask Him to give you clarity on a troubling situation.

*All-powerful God, You are my Rock, my ever-present
Helper, the Great One who sustains me.*

Reflections

But God...

*You intended to harm me, but God intended it
for good to accomplish what is now being done,
the saving of many lives.*

GENESIS 50:20 (NIV)

———————

Throughout the Bible, there are dozens of verses with the words "but God." Each is a testament to His power to intervene and make the impossible possible, to give strength where there was weakness. If you find yourself making excuses in your life, thinking, *I want to do this, but*... add God to your statement and invite His power to overcome your doubt.

*Lord, sometimes I feel powerless, but then I remember
You are with me. You make all things possible.*

Reflections

Follow Your Star

When they saw the star, they were overjoyed.

MATTHEW 2:10 (NIV)

Do you long for an epiphany? Are you ready to make a big change in your life? Look up at the night sky and ask God for guidance. Be willing to follow whatever instructions or journey of discovery that God lays out before you.

Heavenly Father, I long for an "aha" moment that reveals Your presence. Show me my life's purpose.

Reflections

Loving Your Enemies

*But I tell you, love your enemies and pray
for those who persecute you.*

MATTHEW 5:44 (NIV)

If you struggle with this verse, you are not alone. God asks you to forgive as He forgives, to love as He loves. Every conflict is a chance to become a peaceful, forgiving person. Every dispute is an opportunity to make things better, to feel God's love flow through you.

Heavenly Father, help me to reflect Your patience and kindness in my relationships. Help me bring the light of Your love into the lives of those around me.

Reflections

No Complaints

Moses also said, "You will know that it was the LORD when he gives you meat to eat in the evening and all the bread you want in the morning, because he has heard your grumbling against him. Who are we? You are not grumbling against us, but against the LORD."

EXODUS 16:8 (NIV)

———————

Today, start a complaint diet. Commit to cutting back and ultimately ridding yourself of the unhealthy habit of grumbling. Whenever you find yourself moaning, be silent, or better yet, thank Jesus instead.

Dear Lord, thank You for helping me focus on gratitude over grumbling.

Reflections

No Proof, No Doubt

*Then Jesus told him, "Because you have seen
me, you have believed; blessed are those who
have not seen and yet have believed."*

JOHN 20:29 (NIV)

Thomas had his doubts resolved by a personal visit from Jesus. Yet when most of us face a dark night of the soul, we must forge ahead with less dramatic proof. Through faith we can surpass our doubts, and we can know with confidence that when we seek God, we find Him.

*My Lord and My God, help my unbelief!
When my faith falters, help me believe.*

Reflections

God Is on Your Side

*You keep track of all my sorrows. You
have collected all my tears in your bottle.
You have recorded each one in your book.*

PSALM 56:8 (NLT)

If you feel alone with your sorrow or problems—as if
no one seems to understand—tell God. He understands.
God has compassion for each and every one of us. He is
there to hear you and comfort you. He is on your side.

*Heavenly Father, thank You for understanding
me, for listening, and for guiding me
to look beyond my problems.*

Reflections

Perseverance Wins

*Come, let us go up to the mountain of the L<small>ORD</small>,
to the temple of the God of Jacob. He will teach us
his ways, so that we may walk in his paths.*

ISAIAH 2:3 (NIV)

P<small>ERSEVERANCE</small> always wins. If you are having difficulty
with some unreachable star, some unrelenting problem,
or a goal that seems impossibly far away, don't lose faith.
Keep going, keep praying, and you'll come out a victor.

Lord, lead me to greater and greater things.

Reflections

Always a Student

And he opened his mouth and taught them.

MATTHEW 5:2 (ESV)

———————

Jesus wants you to be a disciple, to keep learning and following Him throughout your life. He wants you to grow your mind and develop new skills that will help you be ready for any challenge. God wants to bless you with wisdom.

Lord Jesus, deepening my faith is a blessed,
lifelong journey. Thank You for being
the greatest Teacher of all time.

Reflections

Do You Shine?

The people who walked in darkness have seen
a great light. For those who lived in a land of
deep shadows—light! sunbursts of light!

ISAIAH 9:2 (MSG)

In times when you feel like you're walking in darkness, ask yourself: Do I shine? Does my faith and ability to trust Jesus draw others toward Him? Is my positive attitude a beacon of His light? If you answered no, think of this verse, take a moment, and breathe deeply as you imagine God's light flowing through you.

Lord Jesus, show me where I can shine
more brightly for You today.

Reflections

The Path to Joy

I pondered the direction of my life, and I turned to follow your laws. I will hurry, without delay, to obey your commands.

PSALM 119:59–60 (NLT)

T oday, pray the above verse and ponder the direction you're headed. Know that God listens to His Word as you pray it back to Him. He cares how you apply His lessons to your life. Living by His Word and walking with Jesus is the path to joy.

Heavenly Father, I turn to follow Your commands.

Reflections

Live Victoriously

*But of that day and that hour knoweth no
man, no, not the angels which are in heaven,
neither the Son, but the Father.*

MARK 13:32 (KJV)

At any minute, the world as you know it could change
abruptly. Jesus warns in Mark to be on alert. Live each
day fully, serving and praising God. Be grateful for all
His gifts and trust Him implicitly with your future.

*Heavenly Father, teach me to bring blessings to
others and find peace as I walk with You each day.*

Reflections

Remove the Veil

*So all of us who have had that veil removed can see
and reflect the glory of the Lord. And the Lord—who
is the Spirit—makes us more and more like him as
we are changed into his glorious image.*

2 CORINTHIANS 3:18 (NLT)

When you look in the mirror, what do you see? God
wants you to remove the veil so that you can see what He
sees. As His follower, the more you look with His vision,
the more you believe in Him and reflect His image.

*Lord, thank You for creating me in Your image.
I long to see as You see and to love as You love.*

Reflections

The Answer to All Your Prayers

*Then when you call, the Lord will answer.
"Yes, I am here," he will quickly reply.*

ISAIAH 58:9 (NLT)

Is an unanswered prayer weighing on your heart? Know that sometimes God answers prayers not with solutions, or new situations, but by giving Himself—by being there. Think of your unanswered prayer and then feel His spirit descending on you. Listen for His words: *Yes, I am here.*

Lord God, Your presence answers all my prayers.

Reflections

Rich Beyond Measure

*There is that maketh himself rich, yet hath nothing:
There is that maketh himself poor, yet hath great riches.*

PROVERBS 13:7 (KJV)

Norman Vincent Peale famously said, "Empty pockets never held anyone back. Only empty heads and empty hearts can do that." Some of us spend so much energy and worry over our bank accounts when the richest experience in life—a strong relationship with God—cannot be bought. And if you don't have faith, all the money in the world will not fill the void.

*Lord, my relationship with You, and all the
blessings that flow because of my faith,
make me rich beyond worldly measure.*

Reflections

God's Creation

*Who has believed our message and to whom
has the arm of the Lord been revealed?*

ISAIAH 53:1 (NIV)

Who set this universe in motion? Who arranged it all?
Happenstance? Evidence of God is all around us—from
the perfection of an infant to the beauty of a sunrise.
Today, awaken your heart to the everyday miracles of
God's creation.

*Lord, thank You for the boundless beauty, love,
and blessings You shower upon us.*

Reflections

Are You on the Right Road?

*Enter through the narrow gate. For wide is the gate
and broad is the road that leads to destruction, and
many enter through it. But small is the gate and narrow
the road that leads to life, and only a few find it.*

MATTHEW 7:13–14 (NIV)

———

Jesus spoke of two roads: the hard-to-find, narrow gate
that leads to eternal life and the popular, wide gate that
leads to destruction. Are you on the right road? The
journey is not always easy on the less popular route, but
the trip is filled with meaning and the view is heavenly!

Lord, I am so thankful to be on this journey with You.

Reflections

Be Gentle with Yourself

*And so we know and rely on the love God has
for us. God is love. Whoever lives in love lives
in God, and God in them.*

1 JOHN 4:16 (NIV)

The next time you're comparing yourself to another
person, or obsessing over a goal yet to be reached, turn
to the above verse and know that Jesus sees you—every
single perfectly imperfect part of you—and loves you. He
not only sees you as you truly are, but as the person He
created you to be… and is helping you become.

*Heavenly Father, today I will try to be kind to myself,
to let go of judgment and rest in Your love.*

Reflections

Go Forward with Love

*Remember not the former things, nor consider the
things of old. Behold, I am doing a new thing; now
it springs forth, do you not perceive it? I will make a
way in the wilderness and rivers in the desert.*

ISAIAH 43:18–19 (ESV)

Ask God to help you leave behind barriers that block
you from having a closer relationship with Him and
look to the future. Let go of what is impeding you from
living your best full life and go forward on the path He
clears for you.

*Heavenly Father, release me of thoughts and things
that get in the way of our relationship.*

Reflections

Calm Your Nerves

*And the peace of God, which transcends
all understanding, will guard your hearts
and your minds in Christ Jesus.*

PHILIPPIANS 4:7 (NIV)

When you feel anxious, say this verse silently in your mind. Let its meaning sink into your thoughts. Contemplate the vast peace of God, which is so deep that you cannot fully comprehend it, yet it floods into your life with such force that it leaves you calm and in control.

*God of Peace, flow through me. Calm my mind
and soothe my heart.*

Reflections

The Master Carpenter

*When the Sabbath came, he began to teach in the
synagogue, and many who heard him were amazed.
"Where did this man get these things?" they asked.
"What's this wisdom that has been given him? What
are these remarkable miracles he is performing? Isn't
this the carpenter?..." And they took offense at him.*

MARK 6:2–3 (NIV)

Jesus skillfully constructs our lives. All of our experiences serve the purpose of shaping us into our best
selves—sanding away the rough edges and smoothing
out our character. He invests His time, love, and tender
care in completing each and every one of us.

*Lord Jesus, You are the Master Carpenter
shaping us into works of art.*

Reflections

Find Your Way Forward

*He is the one we proclaim, admonishing and
teaching everyone with all wisdom, so that we
may present everyone fully mature in Christ.*

COLOSSIANS 1:28 (NIV)

Is there an upsetting situation in your life that seems
impossible to change? Often by stepping outside the
drama and looking at the situation from all angles, you
can release your feelings of anger or judgment. Even a
slight shift in perspective can be a catalyst to harmony.

*Heavenly Father, thank You for helping me view the
difficult situations in my life through a wider lens.*

Reflections

Notice His Handiwork

And he did not do many miracles there
because of their lack of faith.

MATTHEW 13:58 (NIV)

What is blocking you from experiencing God's blessings?
Is it unbelief? Every person has moments of doubt when
we can't see or don't notice the signs of His handiwork
in our lives. God doesn't love us less during seasons of
doubt. He is teaching us to walk by faith.

Heavenly Father, when my faith wavers, help me to
stand firmly and trust You over my questions and doubts.

Reflections

Faithful Stewards of God's Grace

*As each has received a gift, use it to serve one another,
as good stewards of God's varied grace.*

1 PETER 4:10 (ESV)

Wasting the gifts God has given us is one of life's great tragedies. Most of us have many talents to offer, but unless we focus on them and ask God for help in applying our gifts to help others, no one will ever benefit.

Lord, when I am feeling confused about where to apply my efforts, help me pick a course and take the first step.

Reflections

Begin with Praise

I have loved you with an everlasting love;
I have drawn you with unfailing kindness.

JEREMIAH 31:3 (NIV)

Do you organize your prayer time with intention? Begin with praise. Praise Him for restoring your spirit and for being able to redeem every situation—for converting your challenges into positive growth.

Heavenly Father, thank You for giving me
so many reasons to praise You.

Reflections

Give Up Control

*The king's heart is a stream of water in the hand
of the Lord; he turns it wherever he will.*

PROVERBS 21:1 (ESV)

Some things in life are simply beyond our control. As
much as we might want something, we can't always
make it happen. We can do our part, and yet ultimately
there are times when we have to adopt a "wait and see"
approach. Letting life unfold by releasing the outcome
to God is a gift you can give yourself.

*Lord, when I release my grip on the outcome, I feel my-
self relax, knowing You are in control. Because of You I
can breathe in the peace of the present moment.*

Reflections

Look to Yourself

*Judge not, that you be not judged. For with the
judgment you pronounce you will be judged, and
with the measure you use it will be measured to you.*

MATTHEW 7:1–2 (ESV)

———◆———

Jesus speaks against judging someone while over-
looking your own faults. Instead of criticizing another,
explore your motivation. Are you being helpful or
hurtful? The Bible tells us only God is able to judge
someone's heart.

*Heavenly Father, help me to steer away from
judgment. Help me to love with my whole heart.*

Reflections

Your Stone of Support

DAY
255

Then Samuel took a stone and set it up between Mizpah and Shen. He named it Ebenezer, saying, "Thus far the Lord has helped us."

1 SAMUEL 7:12 (NIV)

Jesus is your Ebenezer, your stone of support. Imagine that each time Jesus helps you, you receive a special stone. Create an altar in your mind's eye of all these stones and turn to it when your faith wavers. Know that He is your rock. He has helped you before and He will help you again.

All-Powerful Lord, You are my Help, my Savior.

Reflections

Make Peace with Unanswered Questions

You said, "Listen now, and I will speak; I will question you, and you shall answer me."

JOB 42:4 (NIV)

Job longed to understand God's actions. Often when difficult times befall us, like Job, we want answers. "Why did this happen?" Faith will lead us to recognize that we can know and love God, yet we must also recognize that all of our questions will not be answered.

Heavenly Father, help me to find peace with all that is unanswered in my life.

Reflections

Pray Little Prayers

The LORD directs the steps of the godly.
He delights in every detail of their lives.

PSALM 37:23 (NLT)

God wants you to talk to Him about everything—not just the big stuff, but the little things, too. Pray about finding a parking spot or what to have for dinner. Don't worry that something is too small to bother him about. Truth is, God is always happy to hear from you.

Heavenly Father, thank You for being there
and caring about life's little things.

Reflections

Focus on the Good

*Do not be conformed to this world, but be transformed
by the renewal of your mind, that by testing
you may discern what is the will of God,
what is good and acceptable and perfect.*

ROMANS 12:2 (ESV)

Actions are born from thoughts. If you can focus on good things and block thoughts that lead to destructive behavior, you can break the chain of bad habits and actions. If you can't totally prevent a negative thought from entering your mind, you can refuse to dwell on it and stop it in its tracks before your actions follow.

*Dear Lord, when a negative thought comes to mind,
guide me to follow Your will and focus on
what is good, acceptable, and perfect.*

Reflections

Your Heart: Christ's Home

I pray that from his glorious, unlimited resources he will empower you with inner strength through his Spirit. Then Christ will make his home in your hearts as you trust in him. Your roots will grow down into God's love and keep you strong.

EPHESIANS 3:16–17 (NLT)

Knowing Jesus on a deeper level means sharing your heart and making more room for Him in your life. Today, meditate on this verse and the beautiful truth that Jesus lives in your heart. He empowers you with His strength, love, and wisdom. He fills you with peace.

Lord Jesus, keep me rooted in Your love.

Reflections

No Place for
Lukewarm Faith

*I know your deeds, that you are neither cold nor hot.
I wish you were either one or the other! So, because
you are lukewarm—neither hot nor cold—I am
about to spit you out of my mouth.*

REVELATION 3:15–16 (NIV)

God doesn't want your spirit to be lukewarm. He wants you to live a full life with a full heart. He wants you to be enthusiastic about your faith and excited for the opportunity to delve deeper into His Word.

*Lord Jesus, I come to You with an open heart.
Let me live passionately for You.*

Reflections

Don't Go to Sleep Angry

*Let not the sun go down upon your wrath:
Neither give place to the devil.*

EPHESIANS 4:26–27 (KJV)

Y ou've probably heard the relationship advice, "Don't go to bed angry," and the verse above shows that it dates back to biblical times. Scientific studies back it up. Research suggests that going to bed angry actually preserves the emotion and makes it take root deeper. So the next time anger finds a place in your heart, make an effort to nip it before bedtime.

Dear Lord, the next time that I am angry, instead of holding a grudge, I will pray to You to release the situation through the power of forgiveness.

Reflections

Knowing God's Will

So Gideon said to God, "If You will save Israel by my hand as You have said—look, I shall put a fleece of wool on the threshing floor; if there is dew on the fleece only, and it is dry on all the ground, then I shall know that You will save Israel by my hand, as You have said."

JUDGES 6:36–37 (NKJV)

How can we be sure of God's will? Seldom do we receive signs as clear as Gideon's wet fleece, but given time and patience, we can receive guidance from the small voice that prompts all who listen. If you have a difficult decision, petition God for help.

Help me wait patiently, Lord, when problems appear and ready answers aren't available. Guide me with clear instruction.

Reflections

You Are God's Child

*And a voice from heaven said, "This is my dearly
loved Son, who brings me great joy."*

MATTHEW 3:17 (NLT)

On stressful days, you might feel as if no one under-
stands what you're going through. God knows! You are
His child, and He knows you better than anyone else.
Rest in His presence and soak up His infinite love.

*Almighty Father, thank You for letting me lean on
You. Fill my heart with Your healing love and
the power of Your strength. Take me in
Your loving arms and give me peace.*

Reflections

Use Your Gifts

For whoever has will be given more,
and they will have an abundance.

MATTHEW 25:29 (NIV)

In Christ's parable of the talents, the servants who used what they were given to create prosperity for themselves were given even more money at the end. The lesson we can take from that is that when it comes time to sum up our lives, the only standard that counts is how well we measure up to our own potential. Christ wants us to invest the gifts He has given us by serving and giving to others without restraint.

Dear God, please guide me to give
my gifts without restraint.

Reflections

Trust His Timing

*But God remembered Noah and all the wild animals
and the livestock that were with him in the ark, and he
sent a wind over the earth, and the waters receded.*

GENESIS 8:1 (NIV)

Are you going through a difficult time? Do you feel
that God has forgotten you? Maybe you feel that there's
no end in sight, or no hope. Think of Noah, stuck in the
ark for months, and have faith in God's timing and reasons, even if the specifics are beyond our understanding.

*Dear Lord, I know You haven't forgotten me.
I trust Your timing and Your plan.*

Reflections

Make Amends

*Be kind to one another, tenderhearted, forgiving
one another, as God in Christ forgave you.*

EPHESIANS 4:32 (ESV)

Is there a relationship in your life that needs mending?
Have you let something petty get in the way of having
closer relationships? If you'd like to let go of a grudge,
ask yourself if love can heal the issue. If the person were
no longer in your life, would you regret not making
amends? The time to cut through grievances and heal
hurt feelings is now.

*Heavenly Father, guide me to let go of bitterness
and anger. Help me to be compassionate and
loving, forgiving others as You forgive me.*

Reflections

Angels Watch Over You

*For he will order his angels to protect
you wherever you go.*

PSALM 91:11 (NLT)

———————✦———————

Tuck this beautiful verse into your heart. God is watching over you to keep you in all your ways. His amazing kindness surrounds and guides you. You can go through life with a contented spirit, knowing God watches over you—no matter what comes your way.

*Thank You, Father. No matter how alone or lost
I feel, You know where I am, and your angels
guide me to follow Your direction.*

Reflections

Weighed in the Balance

You have been weighed on the scales and found wanting.

DANIEL 5:27 (NIV)

Is there a behavior or belief that is getting in the way of you living your best life? In what areas are you a spiritual lightweight? When your heart belongs to Jesus, you don't need to worry about being weighed on God's balances and coming up short.

Dear Lord, I praise You for the wholeness I feel because of Your presence in my life. Thank You for saving me.

Reflections

Believe and You Will See

*"Go," he told him, "wash in the Pool of Siloam"
(this word means "Sent"). So the man went
and washed, and came home seeing.*

JOHN 9:7 (NIV)

In the above verse, Jesus directed the blind man to go
into the water without explanation. The man followed
His words and both his physical and spiritual eyes were
opened. When you have the faith to follow God's divine
instructions—not because of an end goal, but because
you believe and trust His guidance—you experience the
blessing of spiritual sight.

*Dear Lord, I long to trust and obey You. Give me
a humble heart to follow Your instructions.*

Reflections

This Blessed Moment

Do not say, "Why were the old days better than these?" For it is not wise to ask such questions.

ECCLESIASTES 7:10 (NIV)

M ost people spend a lot of time reliving the past or fast-forwarding to the future with a focus on what might happen—all the while squandering the gift of the moment. Make right now your focus. Appreciate where you are, and be grateful that you are here.

Heavenly Father, this is the first minute of the rest of my life.

Reflections

God Will Catch You

But when he saw the strong wind and the waves, he was terrified and began to sink. "Save me, Lord!" he shouted.

MATTHEW 14:30 (NLT)

Do you ever have the feeling that you're in over your head? Maybe an unexpected bill or a phone call with bad news sends you into a tailspin. Like Peter in the above verse, when you are frightened or worried, it's okay to cry out to the Lord and know that He will stretch out His hand and catch you.

Father, replace my fears with the belief in Your ability to see me through life's challenges.

Reflections

Don't Be Distracted

*But as for me, it is good to be near God. I have made the
Sovereign LORD my refuge; I will tell of all your deeds.*

PSALM 73:28 (NIV)

———————————◆———————————

Do you spend quiet time with God every day? Schedule
time when distractions aren't likely to happen—perhaps
early in the morning, or at another time when you're
able to turn off your phone, close the door, and be near
Jesus. You'll be amazed at the difference this time makes
in your life, from hearing His whispers to being filled
with His peace and comfort—before long, you'll find it's
a favorite part of your day.

*Thank You, Lord, for showing me the beauty of
Your love in the moments we share.*

Reflections

Jesus's Voice

*My sheep recognize my voice. I know them,
and they follow me.*

JOHN 10:27 (MSG)

Do you hear Jesus speaking to you? His voice is clear and concise, for He is Lord of peace and order (1 Corinthians 14:33). His voice encourages you to grow and become stronger and greater. He is perfect love who drives out fear (1 John 4:18). His messages soothe and comfort. He leads and forgives. Focus on these attributes and delve into His Word to hear Him accurately.

*Heavenly Father, help me discern
Your voice in my mind's chatter.*

Reflections

Comfort from Heaven

*Jesus said to her, "I am the resurrection and the life.
The one who believes in me will live, even though
they die; and whoever lives by believing in me
will never die. Do you believe this?"*

JOHN 11:25–26 (NIV)

For those missing a loved one in heaven, take comfort knowing that someday you will be reunited with them. Norman Vincent Peale said, "Darkness is powerless before the onslaught of light. And so it is with death. We have allowed ourselves to think of it as a dark door, when actually it is a rainbow bridge spanning the gulf between two worlds."

*Our Heavenly Father, thank You for this
great truth that life and love are everlasting.*

Reflections

I'm Ready to Help

*Therefore encourage one another
and build each other up.*

1 THESSALONIANS 5:11 (NIV)

Busy times and long days make it easy to overlook other people's needs. But if you embrace God's command in the above verse, your actions can have a lasting impact in another's life. Look for ways to be a blessing to others. Simple and small gestures can make a world of difference.

*Heavenly Father, make me aware of anyone
who needs prayer. Guide me to a friend that
needs encouragement. I'm ready to help.*

Reflections

Your Spiritual Vision

*But blessed are your eyes because they see,
and your ears because they hear.*

MATTHEW 13:16 (NIV)

When you submerge yourself in God's Word and His teachings, your spiritual eyes are refocused and renewed. Your life's path has a new sense of clarity, and you gain a fresh perspective on what is important. Ask God to help you select a verse that will guide you and enhance your vision today.

Lord Jesus, give me "new eyes" so that I can see as You do. Eyes that are open and focused on what You want me to see and do today.

Reflections

Love Your Shape

*So God created human beings in his own image. In the
image of God he created them; male and female
he created them. . . . Then God looked over all he had
made, and he saw that it was very good!*

GENESIS 1:27, 31 (NLT)

If you are ever tempted to look in the mirror and judge
your reflection, shift your focus to the above verse. If you
find yourself being critical, recognize that God designed
every part of you. You are His masterpiece! You are His
child.

*Dear Lord, guide me to see the beauty that
You created in me.*

Reflections

Give God Your Worry List

*Therefore, I tell you, do not worry about your life,
what you will eat or drink; or about your body,
what you will wear. Is not life more than food,
and the body more than clothes?*

MATTHEW 6:25 (NIV)

Is your faith cloaked in fear? Do you worry about big things and little things, going over worst-case scenarios when faced with a challenge? In the above verse, Jesus tells us not to worry. Worry is a choice—a wrong choice. Instead, focus your trust in Him.

*Dear God, I give You my worry list so that
You may give me Your peace.*

Reflections

His Love Endures Forever

*Oh, give thanks to the Lord, for he is good,
for his steadfast love endures forever!*

PSALM 107:1 (ESV)

God understands everything about you—your passions and goals, strengths and weaknesses—and He loves you dearly. Praise God for His abounding, unconditional, and eternal love. Live confidently, knowing that His steadfast love is constantly flowing into your life.

*Heavenly Father, how great and faithful is Your love!
Help me recognize the mercies and blessings You bestow
upon me today and every day.*

Reflections

The Best Is Yet to Come

Be careful what you think, because
your thoughts run your life.

PROVERBS 4:23 (NCV)

It may sound overly simple, but how you think about your future shapes it. Instead of falling into negative thinking about tomorrow, fill your mind with happy thoughts and positive goals. You will reap the benefits of a blessed future.

Dear Lord, thank You for filling
my future with heavenly blessings.

Reflections

What to Pray For

I will not leave you comfortless: I will come to you.

JOHN 14:18 (KJV)

Today, instead of praying for things, pray for God to flood your being with Himself. Ask Him to enter your heart and fill you with His love. If you do this regularly, your life will take a positive and miraculous turn. Everything will fall into its proper place.

*Dear Lord, come to me and comfort
me with Your peace.*

Reflections

Dry Your Tears

*Praise be to the God and Father of our Lord Jesus
Christ, the Father of compassion and the God of
all comfort, who comforts us in all our troubles, so
that we can comfort those in any trouble with the
comfort we ourselves receive from God.*

2 CORINTHIANS 1:3–4 (NIV)

Elisabeth Elliot wrote, "Repeatedly throughout our lives we encounter the roadblock of suffering. What do we do with it? Our answer will determine what we can say to another who needs comfort." When you are in pain, allow Jesus to comfort you so that you may extend His comfort to others.

*Dear Lord, guide me to see the good in my situation.
Help me to heal so that I may help another in need.*

Reflections

Say His Name

*And this is his commandment: We must believe
in the name of his Son, Jesus Christ, and love
one another, just as he commanded us.*

1 JOHN 3:23 (NLT)

There is great power in speaking Jesus's name. When
you are going through a difficult time or feeling alone
or frightened, simply say His name and repeat this verse:
"The name of the Lord *is* a strong tower; the righteous
run to it and are safe" (Proverbs 18:10, NKJV). Feel His
peace and know that He is with you.

Lord Jesus, Your name is a strong tower...

Reflections

Give Yourself a Life Audit

I beseech you, therefore, brethren, by the mercies of God, that ye present your bodies a living sacrifice, holy, acceptable unto God, which is your reasonable service.

ROMANS 12:1 (KJV)

T he busyness of daily life can rob you of reflection and fulfillment. Don't get caught in the trap of running from place to place without stopping to think about where you are going and why. Today, take a moment, slow down, and consider. Review your priorities in life and ask God for insight and guidance. Are you in the center of His will or have you let other things crowd Him out?

Dear Lord, align my life with Your purpose.

Reflections

Spread Joy

Being strengthened with all power, according to his glorious might, for all endurance and patience with joy.

COLOSSIANS 1:11 (ESV)

———————◆———————

Joy is powerful and wonderfully contagious. The Bible is filled with scriptures that connect faith with joy. (See Nehemiah 8:10 and Psalm 28:7.) Jesus yearns for you to share the joys of life with others. Look for opportunities to raise someone's spirit and give them a boost of energy.

Lord, thank You for the power of joy.

Reflections

Look Forward, Not Back

*Forgetting those things which are behind, and
reaching forth unto those things which are before,
I press toward the mark for the prize of the
high calling of God in Christ Jesus.*

PHILIPPIANS 3:13–14 (KJV)

Memories are great places to visit, but don't dwell there. Instead, heed the Apostle Paul's advice in the above verse. Growing and aging is one of God's greatest gifts. Thank Him for every new day—and then get on with the work that lies ahead.

*Heavenly Father, help me make the most
of every day of my life.*

Reflections

Resist the Negative

*There are six things the Lord hates . . . and [one is]
a person who stirs up conflict in the community.*

PROVERBS 6:16, 19 (NIV)

Some situations and people seem to pull us into negativity—whether it's bad influences, for example, or gossip,
or judging others. If you feel yourself going down the
wrong road and entertaining negative behavior, know
it's okay to set boundaries and say no. Rather than be
pulled into the darkness of conflict, be a gentle guide to
show another the Light.

*Heavenly Father, guide me to see the positive
in others, to mend relationships, and build
strong and loving friendships.*

Reflections

Are You Ready?

*You also must be ready all the time, for the
Son of Man will come when least expected.*

LUKE 12:40 (NLT)

Consider how different your day would be if you lived anticipating Christ's return. Would you greet Him with joy? Would you be proud of the way you're living and how you're spending your time? Are you devoting your energy to the right things?

*Heavenly Father, help me grow in spirit and
understanding so that I am ready for You.*

Reflections

Hope-Filled Living

*May the God of hope fill you with all joy and peace
as you trust in him, so that you may overflow
with hope by the power of the Holy Spirit.*

ROMANS 15:13 (NIV)

Are you worried about the outcome of a situation? Take a moment and shift your thinking. Instead of justifying your fears by wrongly believing that your worry will somehow control what will happen, truly put your faith in God. Replace your stress with the hopeful power of the Holy Spirit.

*Dear Lord, because of You I can be full of hope
no matter what circumstances or outcomes lie ahead.*

Reflections

Complain to God

*I cry aloud to the Lord; I lift up my voice to
the Lord for mercy. I pour out before him my
complaint; before him I tell my trouble.*

PSALM 142:1–2 (NIV)

God wants you to be honest with Him. If you are angry
or upset about a situation, or frustrated and hurt by the
reality that bad things happen to good people, express
your feelings. Share your grief, your concerns. Get them
out of your mind and into prayer.

Dear God, I'm angry about _____,
but I'm thankful that I have You to confide in.

Reflections

Glimpses of His Glory

*Jesus also did many other things. If they were
all written down, I suppose the whole world could
not contain the books that would be written.*

JOHN 21:25 (NLT)

We live in a world packed with God's miracles. Not
just dramatic, once-in-a-lifetime experiences, but small
yet profoundly meaningful moments of God's grace
blessing our lives. John wrote that the Gospels are only
a small portion of the many things Jesus did. When we
open our hearts and minds to His miracles, we witness
amazing glimpses of His glory.

*Lord, because of You nothing is impossible.
Because of You, I believe in miracles.*

Reflections

In Times of Hardship

*Give thanks in all circumstances; for this is
God's will for you in Christ Jesus.*

1 THESSALONIANS 5:18 (NIV)

It may seem strange to be thankful for sorrow and hardship, but even unavoidable and painful experiences have an upside. Difficult times shine a light on what is truly important in your life. They are moments of growth that teach valuable life lessons of compassion, faith, and understanding. Know that whatever you are going through, Jesus is with you.

*Heavenly Father, I am grateful for
Your healing presence in my life.*

Reflections

The Miracle of Prayer

And this is eternal life, that they know you, the only true God, and Jesus Christ whom you have sent.

JOHN 17:3 (ESV)

Communicating with God, whether you are talking to Him or sitting silently and mindfully experiencing His presence, helps you handle any situation and bring divine order into your life. When you pray, you experience the beauty of life as it truly is—infinite and eternal.

Dear God, thank You for the beautiful moments we share—and the miracles You bring to my life.

Reflections

Clear Away Obstacles

*That is why, for Christ's sake, I delight in weaknesses,
in insults, in hardships, in persecutions, in difficulties.
For when I am weak, then I am strong.*

2 CORINTHIANS 12:10 (NIV)

Are you feeling frustrated about reaching your goals?
Take a moment and consider what is stopping you.
Whether it is lack of commitment, perfectionism, fear
of failure, fatigue, or interruptions—whatever—pray
about how to eliminate the obstacles that keep you
from achieving your goals.

*Heavenly Father, give me the faith, determination,
and perseverance to succeed.*

Reflections

A Supreme Act of Faith

Then Noah built an altar to the Lord and,
taking some of all the clean animals and clean
birds, he sacrificed burnt offerings on it.

GENESIS 8:20 (NIV)

The first thing Noah did after leaving the ark was to build an altar and offer sacrifices to praise God. Consider how he must have felt stepping off the ark onto steady ground. Reflect on times in your life when you needed to act on faith alone.

Heavenly Father, I yearn to be as obedient to
Your call as Noah was—to boldly follow
Your instructions and always put You first.

Reflections

Author of Peace

God is not the author of confusion but of peace.

1 CORINTHIANS 14:33 (NKJV)

W hen life seems to be spinning out of control, focus on this verse. Ask the Author of Peace to help you regain your sense of calm. Take a deep breath and rest in the understanding that God provides peace above and through the confusion. He will give you clarity.

Heavenly Father, when I keep my eyes on You, I can relax knowing You have everything under control.

Reflections

Be Happy at Work

*But a doer of the work, this man shall be
blessed in his deed.*

JAMES 1:25 (KJV)

Are you discouraged about your job, volunteer life, or other daily occupation? Try changing your attitude and see if it makes a difference. Focus on your purpose and ask God to fill your heart with enthusiasm. Give your best and trust your efforts have value.

*Heavenly Father, inspire me to find satisfaction
in my work and help me to be grateful for
having the means to earn a living.*

Reflections

Trapped to Triumphant

*Yet as soon as the priests who carried the ark
reached the Jordan and their feet touched the water's
edge, the water from upstream stopped flowing.
It piled up in a heap a great distance away.*

JOSHUA 3:15–16 (NIV)

Sometimes in life when you are faced with a challenging situation, like Joshua, you must obediently trust God and step into unknown waters. When you feel stuck by the obstacles that are holding you back, step forward knowing that with God's help, you can go from feeling trapped to triumphant.

*Lord, my course is charted. Give me the
wisdom and courage to trust You.*

Reflections

No Comparisons

*For with the judgment you pronounce you
will be judged, and with the measure you use
it will be measured to you.*

MATTHEW 7:2 (ESV)

Often it's second nature to judge others, to size them
up and label them as this or that, to compare yourself
against them. Fight the urge to make assumptions and
judgments. Try and see people as God created them.
When you find yourself pigeonholing a friend, loved one,
or someone you run into by chance, take a deep breath
and cover them with love and compassion instead.

*Heavenly Father, help me to accept others
as they are, to see them with Your loving eyes.*

Reflections

One Small Gesture

*A new command I give you: Love one another.
As I have loved you, so you must love one another.*

JOHN 13:34 (NIV)

Do you ever feel at the day's end that you didn't accomplish half of the things you wanted to? No matter what else you do or don't get done, if you take the time every day to do one thing, one simple gesture, that shows another you love them—really, truly love them—you'll know you've made a difference.

*Lord Jesus, today and every day, I will take
time to love with intention.*

Reflections

God's Word in Your Heart

Let the message of Christ dwell among you richly
as you teach and admonish one another with all
wisdom through psalms, hymns, and songs from
the Spirit, singing to God with gratitude in your
hearts. And whatever you do, whether in word or
deed, do it all in the name of the Lord Jesus, giving
thanks to God the Father through him.

COLOSSIANS 3:16–17 (NIV)

Today, select a Bible verse to carry with you. Think about the scripture throughout the day and look for ways to apply His word to "whatever you do, whether in word or deed." Let His word dwell in you.

Heavenly Father, I will keep Your Word in my heart.

Reflections

Blessed Is the Believer

*Yet the news about him spread all the more,
so that crowds of people came to hear him and
to be healed of their sicknesses. But Jesus often
withdrew to lonely places and prayed.*

LUKE 5:15–16 (NIV)

The next time you feel overwhelmed by stress, remember Jesus's example in the above verse. When crowds sought His attention, Jesus frequently slipped away by Himself to pray. When you are upset, take a moment, find a quiet place, and ask Him to calm your troubled heart and grant you peace of mind.

*Lord Jesus, when I am overwhelmed, I can
draw strength, comfort, and wisdom from You.*

Reflections

The Perfect Prayer

I will give thanks to you, Lord, with all my heart;
I will tell of all your wonderful deeds.

PSALM 9:1 (NIV)

O ne of the greatest prayers is "Thank you!" Norman Vincent Peale said, "Let your prayer consist of all the wonderful things that have happened to you. Name them, thank God for them, and make that your whole prayer. You will soon find that these prayers of thanksgiving grow longer and longer, and you will have more and more things for which to thank God."

Dear Lord, give me the vision to see Your blessings instead of my fears. May I feel Your presence in times of worry and remember Your strong desire to protect and guide me is more powerful than anything on earth.

Reflections

The Very Good Life

*And God saw everything that he had made,
and behold, it was very good.*

GENESIS 1:31 (KJV)

———————◆———————

Perfection is an unattainable goal. If you get caught up in thinking that nothing is as good as it should be, focus on this verse. Notice that the Great Creator didn't describe the universe as perfect, but "very good." Your best is always good enough. Let go of perfection. Applaud yourself for very good jobs well done.

*Dear God, help me let go of unreal expectations
and unattainable goals so that I can be fulfilled
in knowing my best is very good.*

Reflections

Amazing Grace

From his fullness we have all received, grace upon grace.

JOHN 1:16 (ESV)

The Apostle John said that through Jesus, we have been given grace upon grace. God showers His grace upon us in a never-ending, constant supply. His blessings and favor flow over us, cleansing and filling us. If you feel unworthy or lacking, repeat this verse and feel His grace flowing upon you, filling you with divine light.

Heavenly Father, each day in my life is a sacred gift from You, filled with grace upon grace.

Reflections

Sing Joyfully

Shout his praise with joy! For great is the Holy One.

ISAIAH 12:6 (NLT)

P raise God and sing Him a new song...even when you don't feel like it. By keeping your faithful eye on the compass of God's Word—and believing that He will bring you through hardship—true joy is always in reach.

Lord, You are my joy. Thank You for showing me that in the midst of trials and difficulties, I can be joyful because You are in my life.

Reflections

Coming to the Rescue

*So you see, the Lord knows how to rescue
godly people from their trials.*

2 PETER 2:9 (NLT)

Are you facing a trial right now? God has the solution to your problem. The rescue He has planned may look very different from what you imagined. No matter what you had in mind, know that His way is perfect. Trust Him.

*Dear God, thank You for answering
my prayers and helping me through everyday
challenges and life's major trials.*

Reflections

Right Where You Belong

I have called you by name; you are mine.

ISAIAH 43:1 (NLT)

Turn to this scripture when you feel as if God is asking you do to something out of your comfort zone. Know that God is with you. He knows your name. He knows your every move. Ask Him to help you surrender your feelings of inadequacy and let go of limiting ideas you have about yourself. Own your God-given abilities and believe that you can do anything He calls you to do.

Dear Lord, thank You for this beautiful feeling of purpose and belonging that You bring to my life.

Reflections

It's Okay to Be Sad

*When I heard these things, I sat down and
wept. For some days I mourned and fasted
and prayed before the God of heaven.*

NEHEMIAH 1:4 (NIV)

Are you feeling down? Talk to God. Be honest about
your feelings. You don't need to pretend that you're fine
when life hurts. Instead, do as Nehemiah did: Cry. Be
sad. Mourn. Grieve. Ask God to help you believe that
tomorrow will be better.

*Heavenly Father, I know You rescue those
with crushed spirits. Wrap Your arms around
me and heal my broken heart.*

Reflections

DAY
310

Pay Attention to Your Dreams

*In the last days, God says, I will pour out my
Spirit on all people. Your sons and daughters
will prophesy, your young men will see visions,
your old men will dream dreams.*

ACTS 2:17 (NIV)

The Bible has many instances of God sending messages through dreams. If you aren't already paying attention and jotting down the spiritual gifts you receive while you sleep, now is the perfect time to start. The more you focus on your dreams, the more likely you will remember them and discover what they mean.

*Heavenly Father, thank You for the comfort and
peace of a good night's sleep. I pray for good dreams
that guide and encourage me to live my best life.*

Reflections

Prayer Changes Things

*She was quick: "You're right, Master, but beggar dogs do
get scraps from the master's table." Jesus gave in. "Oh,
woman, your faith is something else. What you want is
what you get!" Right then her daughter became well.*

MATTHEW 15:27–28 (MSG)

In Jesus's discussion with the Canaanite woman, she
pleads, banters, and bargains, and amazingly, Jesus
changes His mind. This verse lets you know that you can
change the outcome by prayer. But most importantly,
God wants you to know that prayer changes you, transforming your attitude and bringing you closer to Him.

*Dear Lord, I come to You humbly with open arms.
Without Your help I don't know where I'd be.*

Reflections

Should You Fear God?

The fear of the Lord is the beginning of wisdom:
and the knowledge of the holy is understanding.

PROVERBS 9:10 (KJV)

What does it mean to fear God? Author JoHannah Reardon gives her insight: "Fearing God keeps us from fearing anything else. Because God also loves perfectly, we can trust him and know that one so powerful will conquer all else that we fear in the world. Perfect love balances fear."

Heavenly Father, teach me to trust and fear
You, for I know true comfort comes from having
You as a daily presence in my life.

Reflections

Gifts of the Morning

*I, Jesus...am the Root and the Offspring
of David, and the bright Morning Star.*

REVELATION 22:16 (NIV)

Be mindful of the morning. Recognize that there is something quite special about the quiet solitude of the sun rising—something so spiritual it can catch you off guard, and make you take a moment and take in God. Each new day is precisely planned for you to be reminded of His love and care.

*Heavenly Father, a new day is here,
filled with hope, filled with You.*

Reflections

Digital Detox

*Command those who are rich in this present world
not to be arrogant nor to put their hope in wealth,
which is so uncertain, but to put their hope in God.*

1 TIMOTHY 6:17 (NIV)

It is easy to be distracted by technology—a second to check social media or email can turn into an hour of missed time that could be spent with your family or enjoying the beauty that God has placed before you. Make a commitment to unplug during your vacation or family time—and keep it! You won't regret being present in the precious moments that you share with your loved ones.

*Heavenly Father, guide me to plug into my life
and my loved ones and all that is truly important.*

Reflections

Experience God's Power

*But he said to me, "My grace is sufficient for you,
for my power is made perfect in weakness." Therefore
I will boast all the more gladly about my weaknesses,
so that Christ's power may rest on me.*

2 CORINTHIANS 12:9 (NIV)

W hen you seek God's guiding presence, turn to this beautiful Bible verse, which assures us that God's power works best when we are weak. Our own shortcomings can either defeat us or make us aware of God's strength. Invite Him to turn your vulnerability into an opportunity to increase your faith and experience His power in your life.

*Heavenly Father, when a problem depletes my
energy, replenish my spirit and give me strength.*

Reflections

Have Fun!

A cheerful heart is good medicine,
but a crushed spirit dries up the bones.

PROVERBS 17:22 (NIV)

Having fun is an important part of self-care. Make time to do what you enjoy. Go for a hike; call a friend; watch a feel-good movie that makes you laugh; play a favorite song and dance!

Dear God, I need to make time to let go of my work
and responsibilities and simply have fun.

Reflections

Use Good Words

*In the same way, the tongue is a small thing
that makes grand speeches. But a tiny spark
can set a great forest on fire.*

JAMES 3:5 (NLT)

This scripture is a reminder of the power of words—
your words. Despite the old saying about sticks and
stones, what you say has tremendous impact. You can
use words to encourage or discourage, so be mindful of
all you say. Use your words to uplift yourself and others.
Kind words are easy to give and often remembered for
a lifetime.

*Heavenly Father, help me make the world
a better place, one word at a time.*

Reflections

The Miracle of Five and Two

*Then he told the people to sit down on the grass.
Jesus took the five loaves and two fish, looked up
toward heaven, and blessed them. Then, breaking
the loaves into pieces, he gave the bread to the
disciples, who distributed it to the people.*

MATTHEW 14:19 (NLT)

When you feel lacking in energy and resources, or are unable to figure out how to make ends meet, turn to this verse and plan for the best outcome. Remember, if you do your best, you don't have to try to figure everything out because Jesus already has the answer.

*Dear Lord, because of You, I believe in miracles.
I know that when I give what I can, You are right
there with me, miraculously offering Your blessings.*

Reflections

Sprouting in Faith

*Wait for the LORD; be strong and take
heart and wait for the LORD.*

PSALM 27:14 (NIV)

J ust as God's presence is seen through the changes in nature, you can see His work through the seasons in your life. Even if you feel as though you aren't growing, be assured that He is watering the seeds that will bud into fruition. There is always a new season ahead, a season of new beginnings.

*Faithful God, thank You for nurturing my spirit
so that I may blossom into my best self.*

Reflections

A Life of Service

*For you have been called to live in freedom,
my brothers and sisters. But don't use your
freedom to satisfy your sinful nature. Instead,
use your freedom to serve one another in love.*

GALATIANS 5:13 (NLT)

As your relationship with God grows, so does your desire to serve Him. There are countless ways that you can serve God every day. Offer help where it is needed, practice forgiveness, add loved ones and those in need to your prayer list. Devote yourself to becoming an instrument of His work.

Lord, I love You. I praise You for allowing me to be Your servant. Lead me where I am needed. I am here to help.

Reflections

Grow Good Things

My soul, wait thou only upon God;
for my expectation is from him.

PSALM 62:5 (KJV)

Norman Vincent Peale said, "One of the most serious and powerful facts in human nature is that you are likely to get what you are expecting." If you spend years expecting things aren't going to turn out well, most likely that is what will happen. Conversely, if you develop an attitude of faith and expectancy, you will create conditions in which every good thing can and will grow.

Heavenly Father, because of You I can begin
my day with the expectation that I will have a
wonderful day. Thank You for the tremendous
difference You make in my life.

Reflections

Humble Your Heart

*My heart is not proud, Lord, my eyes are not
haughty; I do not concern myself with great
matters or things too wonderful for me.*

PSALM 131:1 (NIV)

Charles Spurgeon said that Psalm 131 was "one of the
shortest psalms to read, but one of the longest to learn."
In the psalm, David tells us that pride causes stress.
When we surrender and let go of things outside of our
understanding or control, we turn to God with humble
hearts and trust Him with the faith of a child.

*Dear Lord, may I walk and grow
with You every day of my life.*

Reflections

The "Lions" in Your Life

So the king gave the order, and they brought Daniel and threw him into the lions' den. The king said to Daniel, "May your God, whom you serve continually, rescue you!"

DANIEL 6:16 (NIV)

In the above verse, Daniel courageously spent the night in the dark den with the lions, and when the king came to him the next morning and asked if God had delivered him, Daniel answered, "My God sent his angel, and he shut the mouths of the lions. They have not hurt me." When you are afraid, think of Daniel and have faith that God will send His angel to control the "lions" in your life.

Heavenly Father, I have nothing to fear with You on my side.

Reflections

Spontaneous Prayer

*Hear my cry for help, my King
and my God, for to you I pray.*

PSALM 5:2 (NIV)

A spontaneous conversation with God, where you say what's really troubling you, is a great way to clear your mind and hear His voice. Spell out your frustrations and worries. Be completely honest and open. Acknowledge that you depend on Him.

*Heavenly Father, speak to my heart and
tell me what I need to hear.*

Reflections

Have Patience

*But those who hope in the Lord will renew their strength.
They will soar on wings like eagles; they will run and
not grow weary, they will walk and not be faint.*

ISAIAH 40:31 (NIV)

We live in a world of instant gratification, instant answers to our questions, instant communication. So when God's timing is at work, our instinct is to take our lives in our own hands and wear ourselves out with ambition and strife. Be patient. When we wait on God's timing, the ingredients of success and accomplishment will be there.

*Lord, when I am pacing and pacing trying to speed up
Your timing, redirect my impatient energy and help me
enter a quiet, peaceful place . . . and wait.*

Reflections

Send Me!

And I heard the voice of the Lord saying,
"Whom shall I send, and who will go for us?"
Then I said, "Here I am! Send me."

ISAIAH 6:8 (ESV)

The Bible is filled with different people praying the amazing prayer, "Here I am, Lord. Send me." Have you dared to pray this prayer? Of course, it requires deep devotion and a bold, courageous heart—but its benefits are amazing! Be prepared to have your life changed by His grace and instruction.

Dear Lord, here I am. Send me!

Reflections

Spiritual Weeding

Some [seeds] fell in the weeds; as it came up, it was
strangled among the weeds and nothing came of it.
Some fell on good earth and came up with a flourish,
producing a harvest exceeding his wildest dreams.

MARK 4:7–8 (MSG)

Gardens, with their blooming flowers or bounty of vegetables, are a good image for our faith. Has anything crept into your life—material want or an unhealthy habit—that needs weeding out? It's important to nurture your relationship with God by taking out anything that separates you from Him.

Lord, help me weed out anything that is keeping me
from blooming and flourishing the way that You intend.

Reflections

Be Specific

*What do you want me to do for you?" Jesus asked him.
The blind man said, "Rabbi, I want to see."*

MARK 10:51 (NIV)

In the above verse the blind man doesn't simply say, "I want you to help me" or "I want to feel better," he says, "I want to see." Being specific is important when you ask God to fulfill a need. When you share exactly what you want, it shows that you trust Him and that you believe He can help you.

*Dear Lord, I know that You are listening—
and that You hear my prayers.*

Reflections

Turn Resolutions to Answered Prayers

Watch and pray so that you will not fall into temptation. The spirit is willing, but the flesh is weak.

MATTHEW 26:41 (NIV)

Often when we seek to make a change in our lives, we work on it for a while, then gradually forget. Before and during your efforts to change, pray for the strength to stay on track and persevere in reaching your goals.

Dear Lord, I believe that I can do all things because You give me strength.

Reflections

Be the Light

Turn from evil and do good.

PSALM 34:14 (NIV)

———————

When something bad happens, do you complain, dwell on the past, and spread negativity? This scripture tells us to do the opposite; not just to turn away from evil, but to do good. When you encounter anger, jealousy, or hatred, strive to make things better. Bring love and understanding to the problem.

*Lord, restore me with Your peace. When I'm
on the edge of losing my temper, give me
the patience and foresight to return good for evil.*

Reflections

Do Your Part

*Guide me in your truth and teach me, for you are
God my Savior, and my hope is in you all day long.*

PSALM 25:5 (NIV)

When we ask God to change a difficult situation, we
must be willing to give ourselves in any way that might
help resolve it. If you've been asking God to intervene in
a personal problem, don't deny Him your own actions.
He may want to use them.

*Lord, I know You love me and are at work in
my life for good. I am here to do my part.*

Reflections

Restart with Prayer

Commit to the LORD whatever you do,
and he will establish your plans.

PROVERBS 16:3 (NIV)

———————◦———————

Some mornings seem fraught with problems, from burning breakfast and spilling coffee to bigger nuisances like the car not starting. When you find yourself beginning a bad day, stop and pray. Ask for His guidance and blessing. Turn to this verse and believe.

Lord, I'm having a bad day. Please hit
restart on my stress and impatience and revise
my day according to Your will.

Reflections

He Rejoices Over You

The LORD your God is with you, the Mighty Warrior who saves. He will take great delight in you; in his love he will no longer rebuke you, but will rejoice over you with singing.

ZEPHANIAH 3:17 (NIV)

———◆———

Let the above verse sink into your heart. The Lord, the Creator, takes delight in you. He longs to shower you with His love. Focus on hearing His beautiful, soothing voice.

Dear Lord, thank You for being my Heavenly Father!

Reflections

Add a Little Grace

I will open the windows of heaven for you. I will pour out a blessing so great you won't have enough room to take it in! Try it! Put me to the test!

MALACHI 3:10 (NLT)

T aking the time to say grace sets a place for God at your table. If grace isn't part of your routine, start today. Elevate your meal to a blessed moment.

Bless us, oh Lord, and the gifts we will receive today. Help me give thanks for Your many blessings.

Reflections

Maker of Great Endings

*Return to your home and describe what
great things God has done for you.*

LUKE 8:39 (NASB)

Some of life's worst experiences serve as our greatest lessons. Through our struggles, we learn to trust, to have faith, and to recognize God's touch in our lives. Every Christian has a faith story—that "aha!" moment when they first experienced God's divine love. When we share how our faith has helped us through tough times, we share His love and offer comfort to those who need a boost of hope.

Maker of miracles and great endings, may my testimony be a beacon of light to someone in the darkness.

Reflections

The Seven "I Am" Statements

I am the light of the world.

JOHN 8:12 (NLT)

Jesus made seven "I am" statements in the Gospel of John: I am the bread of life, I am the light of the world, I am the gate for the sheep, I am the good shepherd, I am the resurrection and the life, I am the way and the truth and the life, and I am the vine. With these declarations, Jesus went to great lengths to clarify His mission and to help the people understand that He is the Messiah. He is the Light in the darkness.

Lord Jesus, You are the Resurrection and the Life.
You are the Truth and the Light.

Reflections

Fear-Proof Your Day

Set your minds on things above, not on earthly things.

COLOSSIANS 3:2 (NIV)

Are you an overthinker? Instead of releasing your problems to God, do you agonize over solving them, convinced that if you could just figure them out, everything would be fine? This exhausting exercise leaves us feeling spiritually empty. Instead, focus your energy on God.

Heavenly Father, sometimes I need help focusing on You and not my fears. Keep me obedient to You and help me trust Your will.

Reflections

DAY 338

Difficult Love

Jesus looked at him and loved him.

MARK 10:21 (NIV)

Is there someone in your life who is difficult to love? Instead of filling your heart with resentment or anger, ask Jesus to help you release your feelings and see this person as He sees them. Spend time in prayer asking for a bigger heart.

Heavenly Father, open my heart. Help me to love others like You love them.

Reflections

New Life, Right Now

*Don't you know that you yourselves are God's temple
and that God's Spirit dwells in your midst?*

1 CORINTHIANS 3:16 (NIV)

God does everything right. He has given us a beautiful
world. He takes care of us. Watches over us. Sustains us.
When you know that God is your Father and that His
Spirit dwells inside you, life becomes more wonderful
every day.

*Heavenly Father, each day is an opportunity
for me to grow closer to You.*

Reflections

Get Well with the Bible

Those who hope in the LORD will renew their strength.
They will soar on wings like eagles; they will run and
not grow weary, they will walk and not be faint.

ISAIAH 40:31 (NIV)

We all get little illnesses now and then, or maybe feel physically ill due to stress or problems in our lives. Don't underestimate the power of your mind in promoting wellness. Pray, talk, and believe in healthy, healing thoughts; praise God for His healing power. Several times a day, offer up a prayer of affirmation, reaching out to God for His healing and strength.

Dear Lord, I need Your divine comfort.
Please help heal me.

Reflections

Keep Moving Forward

*We share in his sufferings in order that we may
also share in his glory. I consider that our present
sufferings are not worth comparing with the
glory that will be revealed in us.*

ROMANS 8:17–18 (NIV)

When you are going through dark times, keep moving.
Have faith and place your hope in Jesus, the Light of the
world. Know that there is always light at the end of the
tunnel, and every tunnel offers lessons that will help you
grow. Every tunnel moves you forward to a destination.

*Lord, it's uncomfortable in the tunnel, but I trust You.
Together we will make it to the other side.*

Reflections

Build Your Confidence

In the fear of the LORD is strong confidence.

PROVERBS 14:26 (KJV)

When you get close to God, your weaknesses, self-doubts, and insecurities disintegrate. As a child of God, you have the strength within you to meet any situation. Make a plan for what you aspire to be and hold it firmly in your mind. Commit your life into God's hands and let Him bring out the powerful person within you who is able to overcome.

Heavenly Father, let me feel close to You. Grant,
O Lord, that in this moment I may truly surrender
my life to You and realize the power that is within me.

Reflections

The World's Treasure

And he said to them, "Take care, and be on your guard against all covetousness, for one's life does not consist in the abundance of his possessions."

LUKE 12:15 (ESV)

Some people believe that material things can make them happy, but looking for happiness through objects is a never-ending cycling of wanting more. It may be a cliché that you can't buy happiness, but it's also an important truth. In reality, the true gifts of life come from moments shared and beauty witnessed—laughter with loved ones, a glorious sunrise, a rainbow after a storm.

Dear Lord, all the treasure of the world is already mine—not to own, but to cherish and share.

Reflections

God's Good Work

*For we are God's handiwork, created in
Christ Jesus to do good works, which God
prepared in advance for us to do.*

EPHESIANS 2:10 (NIV)

Today, thank God for working in your life. He is constantly preparing you for moments and situations that are uniquely yours. By engaging in His Word and praying, you have welcomed Him into your life. Rejoice! You are an instrument of His grace.

*Dear Lord, thank You for the good work
You have prepared for me. When I trust
Your plan, miracles happen.*

Reflections

Love Greatly

Therefore, I tell you, her many sins have been forgiven—as her great love has shown. But whoever has been forgiven little loves little.

LUKE 7:47 (NIV)

———◆———

Love and relationships are complicated. Everyone makes mistakes, says things they shouldn't, misses events, and misreads unspoken signals. This verse helps us to remember that loving, trying, and forgiving are all necessary parts of loving greatly—and experiencing God's love.

Heavenly Father, help me to have a forgiving heart that opens me to Your great love.

Reflections

Grace Brings Purpose
to Mistakes

*After everyone was full, Jesus told his disciples, "Now
gather the leftovers, so that nothing is wasted."*

JOHN 6:12 (NLT)

This beautiful verse reminds us that every part of you—
your mistakes and problems—play a role in shaping
you into an understanding, powerful person. All of your
pain and failures equip you to minister to others in sim-
ilar situations.

*Dear Lord, help me use the leftover
pieces of my past for Your purpose.*

Reflections

God Is Present Everywhere

*David was dancing before the LORD with all his might,
while he and all Israel were bringing up the ark of the
LORD with shouts and the sound of trumpets.*

2 SAMUEL 6:14–15 (NIV)

David's dancing in the above scripture is his way of expressing great emotion. He clearly felt God's presence. Have there been times in your life when you felt overcome with emotion by His presence? Perhaps the birth of a child, the beauty of a sunrise, divine comfort during a gripping moment of grief. Reflect on your divine experiences.

*Dear Lord, I am forever grateful to
You for being so good to me!*

Reflections

The Reflection of Your Heart

*But the LORD said to Samuel, "Do not consider
his appearance or his height, for I have rejected him.
The LORD does not look at the things people look at."*

1 SAMUEL 16:7 (NIV)

Today, put as much attention on your thoughts and
feelings as you do on your outward appearance. As you
get ready for your day, check your attitude. Focus on
being authentic and kind. Pray for God's help to develop
a beautiful heart that loves and gives generously.

*Heavenly Father, help me reflect Your patience
and kindness in my relationships. Help me bring
the light of Your love to the lives of those around me.*

Reflections

Sing God's Praises

He put a new song in my mouth,
a hymn of praise to our God.

PSALM 40:3 (NIV)

O ur struggles, our successes, even our failures—these
are not our song. God is our song. When you make time
for Him, putting your faith first, you experience a new
song, a new way of life, a symphony of His beauty.

Heavenly Father, help us to live joyously, to celebrate
the song in our heart and rejoice always.

Reflections

Change Is Good

*For the Spirit God gave us does not make us timid,
but gives us power, love and self-discipline.*

2 TIMOTHY 1:7 (NIV)

P rogress is impossible without change. Yet many fear taking a leap toward something better. Instead, we stay in jobs we don't like or relationships that have problems. If there is something in your life that needs to change, pray. Use this verse as an affirmation to help you have the bravery to move forward. You are not alone. Blessings lie ahead.

*Dear God, help me to face the changes I should
make in my life; grant me the courage to leap.*

Reflections

Pray for Peace

The fruit of that righteousness will be peace; its effect will be quietness and confidence forever.

ISAIAH 32:17 (NIV)

Do you pray for world peace? Sometimes we are so caught up in our own personal needs that we forget to put the power of prayer behind something as large as peace on earth. Today, focus all your thoughts on the people of the world; ask God to give leaders the insight to obtain justice for all. Ask Him to teach us all humility and responsibility to care for those in need, so that the world may be a safe home for everyone.

Prince of Peace, may the oppressed and needy experience justice, equality, and a world without hunger and poverty.

Reflections

Joy-Filled Living

*These things I have spoken to you, that my joy
may be in you, and that your joy may be full.*

JOHN 15:11 (ESV)

———

One of God's greatest gifts is joy. Norman Vincent
Peale said, "There is a human tendency to always think
that we are going to begin being happy sometime in the
future. The right time is now." With faith in the Lord,
your life can be full of joy.

*Heavenly Father, thank You for the gift of joy
that lifts me up and keeps me going.*

Reflections

Crisis of Faith

*The L*ORD *is good to all; he has compassion
on all he has made.*

PSALM 145:9 (NIV)

Has something so tragic happened in your life—the death of a loved one or loss of a job—that you can no longer pray for God's will because you've lost faith that perhaps what He wants is also what you want? If this happens, don't turn away from Him, turn toward Him. Know that He is transforming you. Yes, life can be difficult and break your heart—but it is brilliant and beautiful, too. Trust Him.

Dear Lord, I love You. I want what You want.

Reflections

Take Care of
Your Whole Self

*And the very God of peace sanctify you wholly;
and I pray God your whole spirit and soul
and body be preserved blameless unto the
coming of our Lord Jesus Christ.*

1 THESSALONIANS 5:23 (KJV)

Aligning your life with God's will involves body, mind, and spirit, not just spirit alone. Taking care of yourself physically is an important aspect of your faith. Getting enough sleep, eating healthfully, and exercising—all play a part in taking care of your whole self.

*Heavenly Father, let my life demonstrate
how much You really mean to me.*

Reflections

The Power of the Holy Spirit

I pray that out of his glorious riches he may strengthen you with power through his Spirit in your inner being, so that Christ may dwell in your hearts through faith.

EPHESIANS 3:16–17 (NIV)

True empowerment flows from the Holy Spirit's presence in your life. The very same power that raised Christ from the dead lives in you (Romans 8:11). The Holy Spirit gives you everything you need to nurture your relationships, make wise decisions, break bad habits, and truly live the life you want.

Heavenly Father, I need Your power to help me.

Reflections

Shelter from Life's Storms

*He draws up the drops of water, which distill as rain
to the streams; the clouds pour down their moisture
and abundant showers fall on mankind.*

JOB 36:27–28 (NIV)

W hen life's storms have you feeling like you are in a cyclone, instead of trying to understand or fix the situation, think about this verse. The Lord Almighty can help change your perspective or walk with you through challenging situations just as surely as He showers the earth from heaven.

*Dear Lord, when the details and secrets of life
seem overwhelming, remind me to hold onto You
and take comfort knowing that Your ways are
higher than my ways.*

Reflections

Miracles Designed
Just for You

*He is the one you praise; he is your God, who
performed for you those great and awesome
wonders you saw with your own eyes.*

DEUTERONOMY 10:21 (NIV)

Expect a miracle. Believe God can do the impossible.
The secret behind having a miracle happen to you is simply to be open and ready to receive. Little daily miracles
are often overlooked. Watch for them and be expectant
enough to work for them, and they will happen to you.

*Lord, keep me always with that eager,
trusting, childlike expectancy.*

Reflections

Embrace Imperfections

Therefore, if anyone is in Christ, he is a new creation.
The old has passed away; behold, the new has come.

2 CORINTHIANS 5:17 (ESV)

Nobody is perfect. Yet many of us suffer from negative thoughts about our self-image. Maybe it's our reflection in the mirror, or that nagging feeling like we're falling short on making a special occasion wonderful for our loved ones. The fact is that we are completely beautiful in God's eyes—right now, exactly as we are. He loves and accepts us.

Lord, free me from unrealistic expectations and
unhealthy judgments. Help me to see myself with
Your eyes of acceptance and love.

Reflections

Patience . . . God's Promise Takes Time

Be patient, then, brothers and sisters, until the Lord's coming. . . . Be patient and stand firm, because the Lord's coming is near.

JAMES 5:7–8 (NIV)

Learning to wait is a necessary part of being prepared to receive God's promise. It's not a matter of time, but a matter of trust. When you open your heart to faithful waiting, you pave the way for His promises to work in your life.

Lord God, help me to learn to appreciate the waiting periods and experience every moment in the fullness of Your love.

Reflections

The Source of All Peace

I reflect at night on who you are, O LORD;
therefore I obey your instructions.

PSALM 119:55 (NLT)

A perfect way to calm your mind is to focus on God. Write down a few favorite Bible verses that help you think about who God really is. Quiet your mind and ask Him to help you get to know Him better. Your love and appreciation will deepen as you put effort into truly knowing God.

Lord, I want to know You personally,
as my closest friend.

Reflections

Giving in Faith

*The righteous person may have many troubles,
but the Lord delivers him from them all.*

PSALM 34:19 (NIV)

Sometimes volunteering might seem like a thankless task, but the truth is, when you lend your time and energy, you benefit as well. If you feel like your best efforts are hardly making a difference, remind yourself that every little bit of generosity counts and that you are blessed by caring for others.

Heavenly Father, help me to give in faith.

Reflections

Seek Out Good Company

Do not be deceived: "Bad company ruins good morals."

1 CORINTHIANS 15:33 (ESV)

------------◆------------

Are there people in your life who bring you down, or distract you from your faith? It's important to surround yourself with others who support your relationship with God and, if you've fallen off track, help guide you back in the direction that He has for you.

Heavenly Father, thank You for the beautiful people in my life who help strengthen my faith.

Reflections

Seasons of Change

He has made everything beautiful in its time.

ECCLESIASTES 3:11 (ESV)

The cycles in life, the seasons of change, are completely natural and part of God's order. When you need reassurance and guidance, turn to the Source of all wisdom. He will help sustain you through the ebb and flow of faith and times of uncertainty.

Dear God, I know You will never desert me.
I surrender my troubles to You, knowing that
You will take care of me.

Reflections

Experience True Joy

*The Son is the radiance of God's glory and the
exact representation of his being, sustaining
all things by his powerful word. After he had
provided purification for sins, he sat down
at the right hand of the Majesty in heaven.*

HEBREWS 1:3 (NIV)

K now that God's glory is all around you. He created
you to be joyful and fully alive. Joy doesn't come from
an easy life, but rather from facing and overcoming life's
challenges. Joy comes from trusting and praising God in
every situation.

*Heavenly Father, guide me to make the most of
every day and every situation. Guide me to true joy!*

Reflections

God's Perfect Love Awaits

*I am the Alpha and the Omega, the First
and the Last, the Beginning and the End.*

REVELATION 22:13 (NIV)

As you end the chapter of this year of devotions, be assured that God is infinitely present at every point in your life. He is the Beginning and the End, the One who is faithful all year long. Because of this fact, you can look ahead with expectation and hope, knowing God's perfect love waits for you in every tomorrow.

*Heavenly Father, as one year flows into the next,
Your love is ever-present, helping me to let go of the
past and joyfully look ahead to the future.*

Reflections

About the Author

Sabra Ciancanelli is a writer and editor who lives in an old farmhouse in upstate New York with her family, five cats, and a dog. She holds an MFA in creative writing and has been a contributor to the annual devotional book *Daily Guideposts* (which recently became *Walking in Grace*), for twenty years. In addition, her work has appeared in numerous Guideposts publications as well as a number of magazines.

People to Pray For

_____

_____

_____

_____

_____

_____

_____

_____

_____

_____

_____

_____

_____

_____

_____

_____

_____

_____

People to Pray For

_____

_____

_____

_____

_____

_____

_____

_____

_____

_____

_____

_____

_____

_____

_____

_____

_____

_____

_____

Scripture Index

A Note from the Editors

We hope you enjoyed *365 Days of Prayer*, published by Guideposts. For over 75 years, Guideposts, a nonprofit organization, has been driven by a vision of a world filled with hope. We aspire to be the voice of a trusted friend, a friend who makes you feel more hopeful and connected.

By making a purchase from Guideposts, you join our community in touching millions of lives, inspiring them to believe that all things are possible through faith, hope, and prayer. Your continued support allows us to provide uplifting resources to those in need. Whether through our communities, websites, apps, or publications, we inspire our audiences, bring them together, and comfort, uplift, entertain, and guide them. Visit us at guideposts.org to learn more.

We would love to hear from you. Write us at Guideposts, P.O. Box 5815, Harlan, Iowa 51593 or call us at (800) 932-2145. Did you love *365 Days of Prayer?* Leave a review for this product on guideposts.org/shop. Your feedback helps others in our community find relevant products.

Find inspiration, find faith, find Guideposts.

Shop our best sellers and favorites at
guideposts.org/shop

Or scan the QR code to go directly to our Shop

Made in the USA
Middletown, DE
07 December 2023

44842034R00212